Also by Cherry Hill

The Formative Years

From the Center of the Ring

Horsekeeping on a Small Acreage

Becoming an Effective Rider

Making Not Breaking

Maximum Hoof Power
   (with Richard Klimesh)

101 Arena Exercises

Horse *for* Sale

How to Buy a Horse or Sell the One You Have

Cherry Hill

Howell Book House

New York

To Russ and Greg

Photographs by Cherry Hill and Richard Klimesh unless otherwise indicated

Howell Book House

A Simon & Schuster Macmillan Company
1633 Broadway
New York, NY 10019

Library of Congress Cataloging-in-Publication Data
Hill, Cherry, 1947–

     Horse for sale : How to buy a horse or sell the one you have / Cherry Hill.

     p. cm.

     Includes index.

     ISBN: 0-87605-989-2

     1. Horses—Buying. I.Title.

SF285.H548 1995

636.1'029'7—dc20   94-40106

     CIP

Manufactured in the United States of America

10 9 8 7 6 5 4 3 2

Contents

Acknowledgments

Thank you to the following photo models:

Laurie Krause	Doug Krause
Rachael Krause	Tyler Krause
Penny Bauer, D.V.M.	Ted Stashak, D.V.M.
Lisa Neiberger	Todd Neiberger
Charlie Currer	Connie Buckley

Thank you to the following equine photo models:

Zanzabar Fox
Top Breeze Derussa
Mito Mikato
Me Brush Conclusive
Vandy's Cinnamon Bar
Pierless
Ben Dickens
Ms. Berry Blue
Seeker
Aria
Doctor Zip
Sassy Eclipse
Miss Debbie Hill
Various mares and foals of Randy Dunn's of Laramie, Wyoming

Thanks to the following individuals for their help with portions of the manuscript:

Julie I. Fershtman, Attorney-at-Law
Dale Segraves, Segraves and Associates

Preface

Whether you are buying a horse for yourself or a client, I advise you to place the greatest emphasis on temperament. I have found that a horse with breathtaking conformation but without a willing and cooperative disposition is usually less than satisfying to own. Look for a horse that *has* character, not a horse that *is* a character. Be sure the horse is honest, keen, and self-confident. Also concern yourself with the horse's health and soundness. Select horses with functionally sound conformation over those with "good looks" but mechanical defects. Try to select a horse that is suited for the purpose you or your client has in mind. Although some horses are so versatile that they can adapt to the demands of many sports, it is usually best to choose a horse appropriately designed for the task at hand. This is especially important for specialized uses such as jumping, upper-level dressage, endurance riding, and cattle events. Whether you are a novice or professional, *always* bring someone more knowledgeable than you are to examine and test ride horses that are in contention.

When selling a horse, pre-select buyers through phone conversations and by the use of videotapes. Try to size up buyers in terms of their experience, aspirations, and personality. Making a good match between a buyer and a horse allows everyone to emerge a winner. When describing a horse that is for sale, give honest, straightforward details about the horse's background: health, training, and temperament. Avoid making predictions about what a young horse will become, such as what his mature height will be or what a good dressage (roping, endurance) prospect he is. Encourage a buyer to examine a horse thoroughly and to have his or her veterinarian examine the horse as well. Make sure the buyer knows the horse is being sold "AS IS" and include that phrase on the written portion of the sales contract.

Whether you are buying or selling via private treaty or are a part of a deal involving agents or auctions, keep your eyes open but treat the other parties with respect rather than suspicion. Don't hesitate to hire a respected professional to help you in any part of the search or business transactions.

Horse *for* Sale

Chapter One

Getting Ready to Buy a Horse

Buying a horse can be an exciting and successful adventure or a nerve-wracking catastrophe. The more familiar you are with the process of buying and selling horses, the better your chances will be to end up with the "right horse." Invest the time necessary to become familiar with all aspects of selection, testing, and purchasing horses. Don't be in a rush. If you approach the selection process in a hurry, you might make an enthusiastic and impulsive but possibly unwise purchase. Plan to take from one month to one year to find your ideal horse. Understandably, if you are currently horseless, one year sounds like a very long time, but you can fill the void and become more knowledgeable about what you want by taking lessons.

The first thing you must determine is why you want a horse. What do you want to use him for specifically? Will the horse be a trustworthy trail companion or a spectacular show jumper? A ranch partner or a broodmare? Your first-time training project or a solid mentor to teach you how to ride? Make a list of the attributes a horse must have. This will help determine your priorities.

THE BENEFITS AND RESPONSIBILITIES OF HORSE OWNERSHIP

Next, become very familiar with the responsibilities and requirements of horse ownership. Owning a horse requires a substantial investment of money, time, hard work, and sincere dedication. Horse care costs have risen substantially in

Are you looking for a working ranch horse?

recent years. The initial purchase price of a horse is just the beginning of your costs. Estimated horsekeeping costs are outlined in the accompanying chart.

You must also be willing and able to spend time attending to your horse's needs every day at least twice a day. You will have to tend to feeding, grooming, and exercise every day, as well as buying feed, cleaning and repairing tack, maintaining facilities, and much more. Many parts of horse ownership require hard physical labor: shoveling manure, toting bales, carrying water, training, and riding. Sometimes you will have to make trade-offs. You might have to give up something you'd like to have or do to ensure that your horse receives proper care. You might have to interrupt your sleep, work schedule, or love life to take care of a foaling mare or an injured or ill horse, or to meet with your veterinarian or farrier. During the winter, when you are least likely to ride your horse, the horse requires just as much care as he does during the summer. Horse owners also have legal obligations to their horses, neighbors, and to other horse owners in the area, as well as to pedestrians and motorists who pass by the property.

Are you looking for a solid mentor to teach you or one of your children how to ride?

Sample Budget
(Per Horse Per Year)

Feed

Hay (20 lbs. per day x 365 days = 7,300 lbs. or 3.65 tons x $120 per ton	$438.00
Grain (4 lbs. per day x 365 days = 1,460 lbs. x $.15 per pound	219.00
Bedding	150.00

Veterinary supplies and care

Immunization	30.00
Deworming 6 times per year x $9	54.00
Dental and misc.	50.00
Farm call charges	75.00

Farrier

Shoeing 6 times at $60	360.00
Trimming 3 times at $20	60.00
TOTAL	$1,436.00

Horse ownership provides many benefits. A relationship with a horse can be very fulfilling without having the complications of human associations. A horse doesn't talk back but does tell you, using body language and other nonverbal communication, how he interprets your actions. A horse will reveal your tendencies and can provide the opportunity for you to become a better person. Caring for and interacting with horses can make you more reliable, thorough, trustworthy, honest, and consistent. People who have difficulty working with other persons often find that a horse can teach them the meaning of teamwork. When you work closely with a horse, it is more like a partnership. Both of you have certain obligations to each other, and when those are met consistently on both sides, there is the potential for a successful relationship.

An honest, trustworthy horse can be therapeutic for you if you are caught up in a hectic pace. Riding can help you shed stress and stop the mental conversations that cause it. Few experiences equal a trail ride in the fresh air, especially if there is gorgeous scenery. However, riding down a road or in an arena can also be enjoyable and beneficial for both you and the horse in many ways. A rein-swinging walk can lull you back into natural rhythms; a brisk trot with its metronome-like quality is invigorating physically; a rolling cross-country gallop can rekindle the sensations of freedom within you.

Trail riding is an enjoyable aspect of horse ownership.

The exercise associated with the care and riding of horses can also add to your fitness. Grooming, cleaning, health care, and riding involve many muscle groups and types of activities; the composite exercise is well-balanced and certainly not monotonous.

While some people consider care-giving a responsibility that must be borne, others see it as an opportunity to nurture. Taking care of a horse's needs can help a person establish good habits and routines and bring otherwise elusive order to a chaotic life.

Horses are a feast for the eyes. They are beautiful to watch resting, grazing, playing, and moving with energy and grace. They provide a valuable opportunity for learning about animal behavior. Their reactions and interactions are fascinating and provide material for stories and exchanges.

Being involved with horses offers social benefits, too. Many local, regional, and national organizations are designed for family participation. Groups are available for all types of horse involvement: trail riding, lessons and clinics, competitions at all levels and types, and groups for "backyard horsemen" of varying interests. Besides providing a great place to share experiences, horse groups are a good place to exchange ideas, form friendships, and create a network for group purchases and business transactions.

CHOOSING A HORSE

Whether you are an experienced horseman or a novice, it is always good to get an objective professional's opinion when you are buying a horse. Whether or not you use an agent (chapters 3 and 10) to help you select your horse, you should always have at least a basic veterinary pre-purchase exam performed (chapter 6). When you ask for professional advice, pay for it and then listen to it! When your instructor or veterinarian cautions you about a horse, it is for a reason. Conversely, if you are given the go-ahead to buy and then you get cold feet, you may not find as good a horse again. When procuring advice, it is best to hire an objective professional rather than solicit recommendations from enthusiastic but equally inexperienced friends. Select a well-respected professional who has no vested interest in the horse sale.

Horses are a feast for the eyes.

Don't buy a rehabilitation case unless that is specifically *the* reason you are horse shopping. It is surprising how many people accept poor health, poor condition, vices, bad habits, and unsoundness in hopes of fixing the problems! In some cases, a horse *can* be rehabilitated and that is very gratifying. In the majority of cases, however, what you see is what you get.

The classic bad match is the green horse/green rider combination. Uninformed parents sometimes buy a young horse for a young rider, thinking they can "grow up and learn together." Nothing could be further from the truth. A novice rider of any age needs a well-seasoned, dependable mount.

When a very beautiful, spirited horse catches your eye, it may be difficult to look at other, less flashy prospects with objectivity because the beautiful horse has captured your heart. When such a horse is young, untrained, or poorly trained and you are inexperienced, it would be more prudent to follow your head rather than your heart. Although you may end up with an older and plainer (but perhaps wiser) horse than you originally dreamed of, the pleasant and safe riding will result in a positive experience. Later, when you are more familiar with training principles, you may be ready to progress to a less trained, more spirited horse.

Stay focused. Keep in mind that you are selecting a horse for a particular reason or performance event. There are many decisions and compromises lying ahead, so it helps if you set your priorities clearly at the outset.

If the overall purpose of the horse is to teach you how to ride rather than to carry you to the winner's circle in the show ring, the selection process will emphasize different traits. If the horse is intended to be a long-term project rather than a stepping-stone, you may need to invest more time, effort, and money in your purchase.

CHOOSING A MENTOR

If you need to learn how to ride, you should look for a well-trained, experienced horse. You'll need a patient horse that knows more about riding than you do. Horses of all breeds and types can be suitable as mentors. Most really good teachers are geldings between the ages of eight and twenty, but that doesn't mean all older horses make good mentors. If a horse has not been properly trained to the specifics of riding, even if he is "sweet and gentle" in nature, he would not be a suitable mentor.

Young horses are usually not suitable as teachers because a young horse's responses are not consistent, a young horse has not experienced enough of the world to be unflappable, and a young horse is not usually physically developed enough to counteract the imbalances and mistakes of an unskilled rider.

A school horse must be patient, willing, cooperative and alert, yet calm. He must be physically responsive to the aids, and balanced and rhythmic in all of his gaits. A very thin-skinned, hot-blooded horse would probably be disastrous for a learning rider, so look for a more tolerant (moderately cold-blooded, thicker-skinned) horse that will put up with mistakes as you develop your rhythm and balance. A tolerant horse tends to go on in spite of the awkward movements of a learning rider.

Choose a horse that is not downhill in its conformation (see chapter 4). A downhill conformation would make it more difficult for you to sit in balance and keep your legs under your seat. On a downhill horse, you will either tend to pop forward with your upper body and have a loose seat or brace your back and jam your feet forward in the stirrups, all of which are undesirable riding habits. A horse with withers higher than his hips will carry you in the center of his back and allow you to develop good balanced riding habits with your shoulders over your hips and your heels under your hips.

Pay attention to the spring of rib, because horses with very round barrels will make it difficult or painful for you to ride and slab-sided horses may make it impossible for you to attain effective leg contact.

A good mentor has no bad habits such as bucking, rearing, shying, running away, balking, biting, or kicking. Furthermore, he should not resist by running through the aids, speeding up, tossing his head above the bit, or avoiding contact by staying behind the bit (see appendix for books on riding and training).

Although a good school horse does not have to be beautiful and fancy, he does need to be sound, relaxed, cooperative, and well-trained. So, if learning to ride is your top priority, don't discriminate against a horse because of such things as his age, color, a short tail, a Roman nose, or blemishes.

When choosing a mentor, look for a patient, well-trained horse like this aged Quarter Horse gelding. Photo: Laurie Krause

Chapter Two

Factors in Selection

Before you begin considering the factors discussed in this chapter, be sure you have made a list of what you will and will not accept in a horse. *Before* you start looking, write a description of your ideal horse, including a list of attributes he absolutely must possess, certain things you cannot tolerate, and other characteristics you could live with or live without.

Price   First you must determine how much you can realistically afford to spend on a horse. Remember, the purchase price is just a drop in the bucket when considering the numerous regular costs required for proper horse care. When setting your initial purchase price limit, ask yourself, "Is this the *most* money I can afford?" Long after the purchase price is but a dim memory, you will continue to pay for feed, tack and equipment, routine vaccinations, deworming, farrier care, dental work, bedding, and so on. Because both Bucky and World Champion Mr. Investment essentially require the same expenditures for proper care, set your purchase price ceiling as high as you can comfortably afford. In horse buying and selling, prices are generally negotiable. So if your absolute top dollar is $5,000 and you see an interesting prospect for $6,500, it may be to your advantage to go look.

Since the drop in the oil market in the mid-80s and the Tax Reform Act (which closed tax-sheltering loopholes), the artificially inflated horse prices of the late 70s and early 80s became much more realistic. What was a seller's market in the 70s and early 80s became a buyer's market in the late 80s. However, because of the low profit they were receiving, in the late 80s horse breeders limited the number of horses they raised, so in the early 90s a shortage of certain horses occurred, especially in the prime age group (four to twelve years old).

In addition, the growing market for horse meat has raised "killer price," which affects the low end of the horse market. In many instances, a killer horse will bring from $650 to $1,000 for meat. Because of these factors, the current horse market is fairly equitable to both buyer and seller.

Prices for riding horses range from killer price to exorbitant. Killer price is based on the price per pound that is paid for horses going to slaughter. For example, at 65 cents, a 1,000-pound horse would bring $650, and that would be the very lowest price you could expect to pay for a horse. However, an entry-level riding horse will likely cost between $2,000 and $5,000, depending on the breed. If you have showing aspirations, expect to pay between $5,000 and $20,000. Specialized breeds and well-trained high-caliber horses command prices up to $100,000 and more.

To save money, should you buy a horse at killer price at a sale barn where horses are sold for slaughter? Or should you buy an inexpensive horse off the racetrack? Sometimes you can find great bargains at these places and save a serviceably sound horse from an early death. More often than not, however, such purchases become very costly once problems begin surfacing.

Estimated Price Ranges

Weanlings	$ 500 to 2,500
Yearlings	$1,000 to 6,000
Two-year-olds	$1,500 to 10,000
Riding horses	$2,000 to 20,000

Begin narrowing the field by considering the following factors that, combined, determine a horse's price. Arrange the list in accordance with your specific situation and needs.

Temperament   The single most important requirement for a novice's horse (and for that matter, anyone's horse) is a willing and cooperative temperament. The horse should be calm and sensible yet keen. A keen horse is alert and ready to work but under control at all times. See chapter 5 for more information on temperament evaluation.

You'll make a better temperament match to a horse if you know your own disposition. If you are very *self-confident* you will get along with most horses, unless your self-confidence comes with a lack of experience and a closed mind; then things could get dangerous. If you *lack self-esteem,* then you will need a kind, submissive, "push-button" horse that is not questioning or challenging. If you are the type of person that *doesn't want to blame the horse*, then you'll probably get along all right with a timid horse but not the average horse that

When evaluating temperament, look for a keen, cooperative horse.

needs to be corrected and tuned up periodically. If *you don't want to punish* a horse, you should avoid a problem horse that would take advantage of you. If you are the type to *blame the horse* for mishaps, then you might do all right with a horse that has definite problems because you will assume it is the horse's fault (which it probably would be) and you will act accordingly. If you are *noncommittal*, then you won't be able to train or correct habits. If you are *scattered or inconsistent*, then you will likely give conflicting cues and have different standards every day. This makes for a disaster with a green horse and can ruin many well-trained horses. You need a bomb-proof horse that is very tolerant of the differences in your emotions and attitudes.

Soundness   An unsoundness is a condition that makes a horse unusable for a particular purpose. For a riding horse, working soundness is essential. An example of a working unsoundness is a lameness that prevents a horse from moving correctly. A breeding unsoundness, in a mare, may prevent her from having a foal, but may have nothing to do with her suitability as a good riding horse. See chapters 4, 5, and 6 for more information on evaluating serviceability.

Blemishes   Scars and irregularities that do not affect the serviceability of an animal are called blemishes. Although they are not considered an unsoundness, they often lower the price of a horse. Old wire cuts, small muscle atrophies, and white spots from old injuries may detract from the horse's appearance and may save you money.

Selecting a Horse for an Event

Type	Temperament	Conformation	Performance	Breeds
Pleasure	Calm, dependable	Well-balanced, smooth, attractive, prominent withers so saddle stays put, good angles and elasticity. Level or uphill topline for comfortable ride	Western Pleasure, Hunter Under Saddle, Trail: Efficient, comfortable mover at all three gaits; low stride, little knee or hock action	Certain individuals in all breeds; most commonly Morgan, Quarter Horse, and certain gaited horses
Hunter	Coordinated, cooperative	Neck must be long and supple and tie relatively high at withers and chest to assure greatest length of stride. No exaggerated knee and hock action, knees must not be set back or over or be tied in	Hunter Hack, Working Hunter: Ability to negotiate obstacles 4' high with balance and efficiency	Thoroughbred, Connemara and certain individuals in all breeds
Stock	Energetic but level-headed, cow sense	Well-muscled hindquarters, good lateral muscling overall, inverted V at chest, good inside gaskin muscle to counteract prominent outside gaskin, strong hocks, rounded croup, short cannons. No massive shoulders or chest, no sickle hocks, no small hooves, no downhill topline	Reining, Cutting, Working Cow Horse, Roping, Gymkhana: explosive bursts, lateral maneuverability, cow sense	Quarter Horse, Appaloosa, Paint, and other stock horse breeds
Dressage/Driving	Keen to aggressive, competitive but tractable	Large size; long, well-set neck with clean throatlatch for flexion, elevated forehand, strong hind competitive legs, good substance of bone throughout. Short back and long underline for increased stride from behind, no long backs or weak stifles. Tough hooves with concave soles, no long, weak pasterns	Dressage, Combined Driving, Eventing: Ability to shift and carry weight rearward for collected movements, high levels of stamina with relaxation	European warmbloods (such as Trakehner, Dutch Warmblood, Swedish, Westphalian), Thoroughbreds, Quarter Horses, certain individuals in all breeds

Animated Show	Alert, flashy, charismatic	High-set, stylish neck with long, well-laid back shoulder, clean free-moving joints. Straight legs with long cannons. Crooked legs result in injury at speed. Walkers can have shorter, steeper croup and more set to hock; others a more level croup	Park horse, Three Gaited, Five Gaited: exaggerated flexion of joints with precision, speed, and cadence	American Saddlebred, Morgan, Arabian, Tennessee Walking Horse
Endurance	Calm but not lazy	Relatively small stature; long, lean muscle type with level croup. Good respiratory system; lean in relation to height; deep hearth girth but not round barrel; efficient radiator; dense, tough hooves	Competitive and Endurance Trail Riding: Long distances over varied terrain, efficient cardiovascular system	Arabian and certain individuals in other breeds
Jumping	Aggressive but cooperative	Large stature; steep croup acceptable and desirable according to some. Long, relatively high-set neck to act as balancing arm over fences. Strong pasterns with not too much length or slope. No small hooves	Stadium jumping, Eventing: able to jump up to 7 feet, high level of stamina and maneuverability at speed	Thoroughbreds, Selle Français and other warmblood breeds. Certain individuals in all breeds

Movement and way of going   Ideally, a horse should move smoothly and in balance, without stiffness and crookedness. Part of this is inherent and part of it comes from training and conditioning. Be sure you assess the horse at all three gaits. How comfortable is the ride? If you are just starting out, comfort is very important, so you might be better off looking for an older model Cadillac than a hot and zippy Ferrari. See chapters 4, 5, and 6 for more information on movement.

Conformation   The overall structure of the horse will determine how smoothly and correctly he moves. The conformation should be suitable for the horse activity in which you are most interested (see the chart on pages 12–13). Many horses, however, are quite versatile and can perform fairly well in a variety of ways. See chapters 4 and 6 for more information on evaluating conformation.

Breed or type   Select the kind of horse that is best suited for your proposed use. If you are interested in breeding or breed association showing, you will need to purchase registered animals. However, in some events, such as dressage,

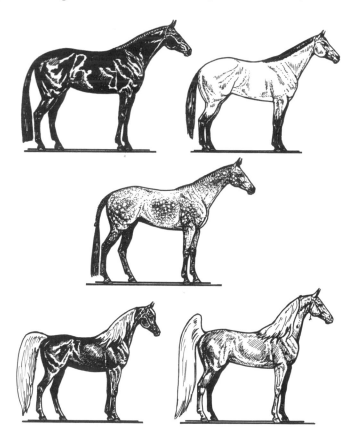

Some types of horses: sport horse, stock horse, hunter, pleasure, and show. From Hill, From the Center of the Ring.

jumping, eventing, endurance riding, and rodeo events, and for some uses, such as ranch work or pleasure riding, a registered animal is really no more valuable than a grade (unregistered) or mixed-breed horse. It is the performance that counts. Since a high-level dressage horse would command a much greater price than a weekend trail horse, a dressage horse would be an unnecessary expense for a casual trail rider. Some registered horses are considered so valuable that they would never be used for ranch work or trail riding. Since an imported registered horse will likely cost many times the price of a locally raised registered or grade horse, be sure you need the expensive horse before you put your money down.

Manners A horse's behavior when he is being handled and ridden, as well as his behavior in a stall or pen, will affect his value. Long-standing behavior is often difficult or impossible to change. Bad habits may lower a horse's price but may provide you with more exasperation and aggravation than the discount is worth. Horses that are difficult to bathe or are slightly grouchy to cinch but perform beautifully under saddle may be an acceptable bargain. However, a horse that turns into a keg of dynamite and refuses to load when shown a trailer may be unusable. A horse that is difficult to shoe can become your farrier's nightmare and a liability for you.

Also remember that a horse's bad behaviors may be at their lowest intensity because of a professional's guidance—the habit may worsen with handling by a novice. Stall vices or bad habits can be dangerous for anyone and should be carefully considered before purchase. Stall vices include but are not limited to cribbing, wood chewing, stall kicking, weaving, pacing, pawing, and tail rubbing. Bad habits include balking, nibbling, biting, striking, kicking, bolting, halter pulling, rearing, and shying. If you are not certain how to recognize these undesirable behaviors, you should take an experienced horseman with you when you go horse shopping. For more information on evaluating temperament and behavior, see chapter 5.

Sex A gelding usually makes the most suitable horse for a novice because castrated males are reputedly more steady in their daily moods. Stallions should never be considered for a first horse unless they are purchased young and with the intention of being castrated and then sent to a professional for thorough training. Mares often make brilliant performers but are often more expensive because of their breeding potential. Also with mares, there can be a period of silliness, irritation, or fussing each month of the breeding season (March to October) due to the hormonal influences of the estrous cycle.

Health Some health problems are temporary, so it may be possible to purchase a sick horse at a discount. The buyer who plans to nurse a horse back to health must realize, however, that what is saved in purchase price may be expended in time, labor, and supplies. There is also a chance that professional veterinary bills will be high, as well as a further risk of complications or the

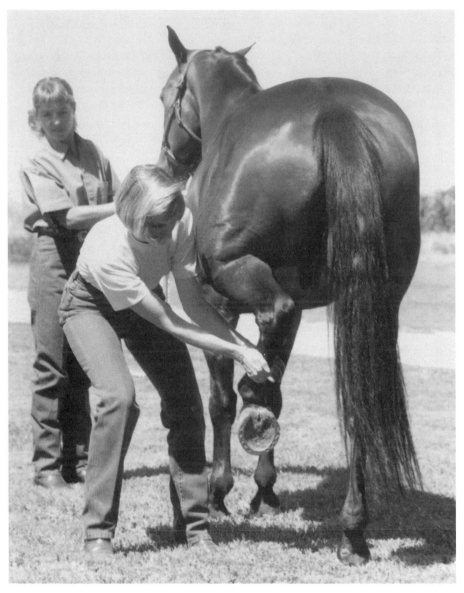

A horse's behavior while being handled will affect his value.

development of a chronic condition. Some health problems are permanent and may require a lifetime of care. See chapter 6 for the veterinary pre-purchase exam.

Age   Trained horses in their prime, five to eight years old, usually command the highest prices. They have matured mentally and physically enough to be useful, have ideally been trained properly, and have many years of service remaining. Very young horses usually cost less because of their lack of training and experience and because of the risk of their developing an unsoundness when put to

Suckling foals are usually lower priced because of the risk involved and the investment required to bring them to riding age.

work. A horse that has been in work and made it past five years of age and is still sound has a pretty good chance of remaining sound. The assurance is not so great with a two-year-old. A sound older horse (over fifteen) may have a few good performance years left and may be the perfect choice for a novice.

When considering a young prospect, it is often helpful to measure the youngster so that you can predict his adult weight and height. The following chart is based on studies of light horses used for riding and driving.

Predicting Adult Weight and Height

Age	*Percentage of mature weight*	*Percentage of mature height*
6 months	45–47	83–86
12 months	65–69	91–93
24 months	87–92	96–98
36 months	95–99	98–100

Larger horses, which mature later, will be on the low end of the range. Smaller horses, which tend to mature earlier, will be at the high end of the range. Draft horse growth rate is much slower than the range indicated. Pony growth rate is faster than the range indicated.

Level of Performance Training and Accomplishments   Here is where the price tag can shoot skyward in a hurry. Training is time and time is money. The biggest test of the suitability and thoroughness of a horse's training is if the horse

There are many horses with fine training that have never been in a show ring.

does what you want him to do when you are taking a test ride (see chapters 4 and 5). A good horse does not necessarily have to have a show record. There are many horses with fine training that have never been in a show ring. They have been trained by people not particularly interested in competition but who use horses for trail riding, ranch work, lessons, or just pleasure riding. Some horses that have been used exclusively in the show ring may be insecure and unsuitable for work in the real world of creeks and trees.

However, if you are interested in showing, you should look at horses who already have show ring experience. A horse capable of performing consistently in the show ring, especially one who has a record to prove it, often commands a higher price. Although awards and points earned in competitions do not tell the whole story, they do highlight a horse as one that has a proven record, not just one that is said to have potential. See chapters 4 and 5 for more information on evaluating a horse's training.

Size Big horses generally cost more, as they can accommodate more sizes of riders. When considering a small horse, be sure to note whether your legs can be positioned properly for effective use of the riding aids. When you are mounted and have proper leg position, your heel should not be below the horse's underline. Ask your instructor to evaluate this during your test ride.

Quality Refinement, class, and presence all increase the price of a horse. The quality horse attracts many buyers. Finely chiseled features, smooth hair coat, clean bone, and charisma all contribute to the horse saying "Look at me!" and, since many people do, the price goes up! Since pride of ownership is a large part of the reason behind buying a horse in the first place, it's nice to own an attractive one.

Pedigree The bloodlines of a horse's ancestors dictate, in large part, his quality and suitability to perform in a particular event. However, using a pedigree as the sole selection criterion is not recommended. Using bloodlines along with other observations can be helpful. Certain family lines become fashionable from time to time and command higher prices. Examples of family lines would be Secretariat in the Thoroughbred breed; Bask in the Arabian breed; and Poco Bueno in the Quarter Horse breed. While all of these stallions sired many performance champions, they sired some poor horses too. First be sure you have a good horse in front of you, then look at the papers. If the horse has famous ancestors, that is a bonus.

Color and markings Although often the first thing one notices about a horse is his body color and points, it is really the least important criterion for selection unless you are considering the horse for use in halter classes in one of the color breeds. Some registries have formed to promote certain color patterns. For example, the Paint horse is a stock type with tobiano or overo color patterns. The Palomino may be of many breeds, but must conform to certain standards of body and mane and tail color. The Appaloosa, Pinto, and Buckskin are other breeds with color requirements.

Chapter Three

Methods of Buying

You can go though the entire selection and purchasing process by yourself or with the help of an agent. If you are inexperienced, you can hire an agent to help with all aspects of buying. (The role of an agent is discussed in detail later in this chapter.) If you have some experience, you might do the initial looking yourself to narrow the field. As you do so, keep a list of all the things you want to ask an agent should you find it necessary to hire one. Be forewarned, though, that if you aren't very experienced in the buying/selling process, you might pass up some very fine prospects. Even if you are very experienced, it is still a good idea to ask someone knowledgeable—your instructor, trainer, or a colleague—for an opinion on the horses that are your finalists. In all instances, be sure to get a veterinary exam.

Horses are generally sold by private treaty, through an agent, at a production sale, at an auction, or via video in conjunction with any of these means.

Private treaty   A transaction in which one person (the owner) sells a horse directly to another person (the buyer). The owner usually advertises the horse and shows the horse to prospective buyers. The buyer makes a straightforward transaction directly with the owner. This form of buying is common for horses of all prices. The seller and buyer both want to avoid the commissions that are added to the price when an auction or agent are involved. However, private treaty is time-consuming and undependable for the seller. A buyer using this route to find a horse often invests a lot of time following leads. Often the buyer pays more for the horse than if the same horse were sold at auction, but, the buyer does have the advantage of dealing directly with the owner without involving a middleman.

Breeding farm or production sale   A one-day affair such as an auction or an ongoing sale of young stock or performance horses. Unless the sale is a scheduled auction, make an appointment to look at the horses. Arriving unannounced is not only inconvenient for the sellers but also may result in your not getting to see any horses. Some farms have ongoing sales and update flyers quarterly. Horses are listed by age and sex with pedigree and performance listed along with the price. Large breeding farms are basically offering a group of horses at private treaty. The obvious advantage is that you can look at more than one prospect at the same location.

Auctions   A combined effort of a sale manager and an auction company (often the same person or company) that present a group of horses to buyers. Sellers choose to use auctions primarily for the convenience. Some people feel it is simply too time consuming to answer the phone and show horses to buyers, and some sellers are too remote to expect to attract many buyers. A few sellers may be trying to get rid of a lame or dangerous horse, or they may be desperate for money and need to sell quickly.

Some breeding farms, like this large ranch in Laramie, Wyoming, produce many foals each year. Suckling foals can be viewed at the dam's side.

Or the entire group can be viewed at weaning time in the fall.

Auctions allow a buyer to see a lot of horses in one place at one time. Many very fine horses are sold at auction each year. And it is even possible to get a bargain if you are smart. Few sales are *absolute* sales, those in which all horses sell, no matter what price is raised. Sales where the seller has the option to repurchase or "no sale" the horse are most common. If the price raised is very low, the seller can say "no sale," pay the consignment fee, and take the horse home.

It is difficult to have a thorough veterinary exam performed at an auction. It is impossible to run an on-the-site blood test for drugs because it takes too long to get the results. However, some auctions offer the following solution. After a buyer purchases a horse, he can have the vet draw a blood sample and freeze it. The buyer pays the vet. If a problem surfaces with the horse within several days, the blood can be thawed and tested. The seller's payment is put on hold until the results are received from the lab. If the horse was drugged, the buyer's money is refunded.

The auction company is the middleman in the sale and the consignor (owner) is not directly involved in the sale to the buyer. Horses are often sold "as is" (usually with limited warranties), with no return. If a buyer is simply dissatisfied with a purchase, he or she usually has no recourse with either the auctioneer or the seller.

This weekly livestock sale consigns low-priced horses, cattle, hay, and tack.

There are various types of horse auctions. The *weekly miscellaneous horse and tack sale* at the local sale barn usually has a low ($25) or no consignment fee. The consignment fee is what the seller pays the auction company to sell the horse. If the horse sells, the auction company also gets a commission on the sale, usually 5 to 15 percent of the sale price. So, if you pay $800 for a horse and the commission is 10 percent, the auctioneer receives $80 of the seller's money and the seller receives $720. Sales such as these generally attract low-priced horses or those heading to slaughterhouses.

A *registered sale* is usually confined to one breed, and depending on the quality of horses, the consignment fee will run somewhere between $100 and $1,000 plus the commission (often 10 percent). A *select sale* is a group of horses that have been previewed (by live horse, video, photos, or paperwork) by the sale manager to meet certain standards before being accepted into the sale. Usually the selection process is completed one to two months before the sale so the sale flyer or catalog can be printed and distributed. Often such sales hold a performance preview the day before the sale. Consignments and commissions of a select sale are similar to those of a registered sale. A *dispersal sale* is a complete sale of a ranch or farm usually as a result of financial problems or the ranch going out of business. Often the sale is held on the ranch or farm rather than at a sale barn.

Auction sales produce a wide range of prices and a variety of sale averages. Here are some actual examples:

This dispersal sale featured a catered sit-down dinner and preview before the sale.

- 42 head from $200 to $10,000 with $1,200 sale average
- 258 head with high-selling horse of $8,100 and sale average of $2,169
- 301 head with top-selling horse $35,000 and sale average of $5,061
- 185 head with high-selling horse $7,300 and sale average $2,141.

It is important to deal with a reliable auction company because you will be assured that you will receive registration papers in good order. Find out ahead of time what type of payment is acceptable. Cash, cashier's check, or money order are usually accepted anywhere. You will need to find out the individual sale's policy on personal bank checks and credit cards. Occasionally, such as at some dispersal or production sales, contracts are offered by the seller to entice buyers. You might have to put 30 percent down and have one to two years to pay the balance at a rate lower than the current bank rate. Of course, if that is your plan, you will need to have your credit approved before the sale.

In some cases, you'll need to register and get a buyer's number when you arrive at a sale. You will need to provide your name, address, and possibly bank information, and show your driver's license. Read very carefully anything you sign when registering.

Terms and conditions   Be sure to read the terms and conditions in the sale catalog thoroughly. They differ from sale to sale according to the state the sale is held in and the rules of the specific auction company. For example, the catalog will state what happens if there is a bidding dispute: two people think they bought a particular horse or the auctioneer calls the horse sold just as your bid is accepted by a bid spotter. Will the bidding be started all over again or will it be reopened at a more advanced bid, or does the auctioneer have the right to settle a dispute as he sees fit? Most catalogs state that the horse becomes the buyer's risk and responsibility at the time the auctioneer's hammer falls; others state it is when the buyer actually signs the acknowledgment of purchase. In some auctions, the printed acknowledgment is passed up to you in the bleachers and in other cases you sign it in the office. Whenever you do sign it, be sure to read it carefully because that is when the title passes from the seller to you.

ITEMS THAT MIGHT BE COVERED IN TERMS AND CONDITIONS (SAMPLES ONLY)

Errors   Every effort has been made to assure correctness of the catalog. Buyers are cautioned to pay close attention to the auctioneer's announcements. All statements and corrections at the sale will supersede the catalog.

Tie bids   If a dispute arises between two bidders, the horse will be put up again for bidding. The consignor shall have the right to pass out or no-sale his or her horse. (Or it might be stated that "This is an absolute sale," which means all horses sell.)

Payments   Cash and payment in full must be made to the cashier immediately after the sale. Bank drafts will not be accepted.

Registration papers   If the buyer pays cash, the papers can be picked up on the day of sale. Otherwise the papers are held until payments clear the bank. The buyer (or consignor) shall be responsible for all transfer and association fees.

Limited warranties   The consignor is the responsible party for all representations or warranties, expressed or implied, concerning the horse. The sales company specifically waives all implied warranties of fitness and merchantability. The consignor warrants to the buyer and XYZ Sales Co. that the title to the horse is free, the animal is sound of eyes and wind, that it is not a cribber or windsucker, has not been nerved or had navicular disease or been foundered, and is not a cryptorchid or ridgeling.

Disputes   If a buyer feels a horse has a particular defect, the buyer has the right to have a veterinarian examine the horse within forty-eight hours of the sale.

Rightful rejection   If a buyer rejects a horse due to findings, the animal will be returned to the consignor and the consignor will refund to the buyer the full purchase price together with all reasonable expenses incurred by the buyer in connection with the animal from the time of sale to the time of return.

Pregnancy status   No guarantee is made of pregnancy status or eventual foaling unless made specifically by the consignor. If a consignor guarantees a broodmare to be in foal, purchaser may have mare examined within twenty-four hours and prior to removal from the sales premises by a veterinarian acceptable to the consignor. If the broodmare's pregnancy status is not as represented, she may be returned to the consignor.

Title   The title to and risk of loss passes to the buyer when the hammer falls. The buyer assumes all expenses upon purchase. All horses must be removed from the grounds within twenty-four hours of the sale.

Coggins test   All horses are tested negative for equine infectious anemia within six months of the sale date.

Bidding procedure   Minimum acceptable advance in bidding is $25 up to $2,000; $50 up to $5,000; $100 thereafter.

Legal   The sale of the horses is governed by the state of _____.

Horses are sold according to the laws that pertain to horse sales in that particular state. Horses sold at auction have not been vet checked, and there may not be guarantees of any kind except as listed in limited warranties. All information that is in the catalog or announced prior to the sale is said to be reliable according to what was told to the auctioneer, but you as the buyer have no recourse against the auction company if the information is not true. So if a mare is said to be pregnant (according to the information given to the auctioneer) and is found not to be pregnant (e.g., within twenty-four hours after you buy her), your only recourse is to go after the consignor. Therefore, you can't rely 100 percent on the catalog or what the auctioneer says about a horse because the auction company is only relating what has been submitted by the buyer. Be sure to look at the horse and have a vet examine the horse if possible. Test ride a saddle horse before you consider bidding on it.

Set a price limit for yourself. Never bid on impulse. Never bid on a horse you didn't examine before the sale but that looks fantastic from the bleachers. Some auctions accept sealed bids or telephone bids, but you will usually be required to send a certified check beforehand to back up your bids. Sealed bids are handled differently at each auction house, so you will have to find out what the specific procedures are. Phone bids offer someone who cannot attend the sale the opportunity to participate in the bidding along with those present.

If at any time during the sale you aren't sure what the bid is or who has it, don't be shy—ask the bid spotter nearest you. If you buy a horse, don't immediately jump up to follow him out of the ring, because the sales ticket might be on its way up to you to sign. Even in your excitement, be sure to read all information carefully.

Make settlement for the horse in the office. Check to be sure your name and address are correct on all paperwork. If you are a member of a breed association, use your name exactly as it appears on your membership. If you are not an association member, you will probably have to pay a membership fee to be able to transfer registration of the horse to your name. Be sure all is in order before you pay your money. In most situations, after you pay for the horse you are given the registration papers and the current transfer form. You pay the transfer fee and send it in. If you pay by a personal check, the auction company may hold the paperwork until your check clears (usually three to thirty days). However, some horses sold at auction have been sold several times without the registration papers being transferred. If the sales management insisted on current paperwork when the horse was consigned, there should be no delays. If not, it might take considerable time and money to straighten this out because all people involved in the previous transactions must be located; they must be current members or pay membership fees to update, and must sign a transfer form in accordance with the rules of the particular breed association. In addition, there can be late fees assessed for transfers that are delinquent. If there is more than one transfer of ownership, the auction company should straighten it out and deduct the fees from the consignor's price.

From the moment you sign the sales ticket, you own the horse and are responsible for providing him with feed and water at the auction facility. You must remove the horse by a stipulated deadline. Some sales make transportation available for buyers who do not bring trailers to the sale. Commercial hauling rates range from 35 to 40 cents per mile per horse for ground transport.

Video sales   Popular vehicles for private treaty sales. Sometimes a sale is made without the buyer actually seeing the horse in person. In other cases the video provides a preliminary means of narrowing the field, especially with very specialized or high-priced horses. As a buyer, you should realize that a video can showcase a horse's strong points but is under no obligation to reveal his faults. See chapter 10 for more information about videos.

An Agent   A professional who helps in the selection and purchase of a horse. When you use an agent, an unwritten code of ethics is in operation. If you understand the basics of buying and selling etiquette beforehand, you are more likely to have a pleasant and productive relationship with your agent.

Before you begin narrowing the field, you need to make an accurate statement of your goals and financial capabilities. This is necessary for your own peace of mind and to provide your agent with essential information, which helps to assure a successful purchase and an efficient transaction. Listen to an agent's or instructor's advice. A certain horse may have great visual appeal but may not be a practical mount. The instructor should be objective enough to see such distinctions. But if the agent (instructor/trainer) and the seller are the same person, do not count on his or her objectivity. Employ another professional for a second opinion.

You must be realistic about price and honest about your budget. If you want a top-class show horse but have a small budget, you must be willing to compromise, usually by investing more and expecting less. Many instructors report that a very time-consuming aspect of horse buying is learning what a buyer really likes. As mentioned earlier, a solution may be for you to do the initial looking. You can take the time to narrow the choices down to what you can afford and would be proud to own. This substantially minimizes the instructor's time involvement. If you use this approach, however, you run the risk of missing a prospect that a more experienced eye might have recognized. Like other professional services, you get what you pay for.

If you have a regular instructor or trainer, he or she will have more long-term incentive to help you find a suitable horse than an agent who is a "stranger" and is more interested in immediate sale profit. Choosing a mount that will work successfully for your lessons is far more important to your instructor than a one-time commission.

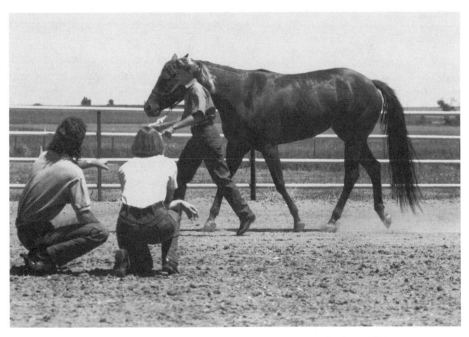

If you use an agent to help you buy a horse, find out what the fee will be beforehand.

If you don't have a regular instructor and need to find an agent, ask for recommendations from respected members of your horse community: stable owners, tack shop owners, veterinarians, farriers, and other riders and students. It is very important to work with an honest, reliable person.

If you get an agent or professional trainer involved in the buying process, you will have to pay for this person's experience and expertise as well as for their time and expenses. You should never expect your instructor to perform valuable horse shopping services without appropriate compensation. Looking at horses, testing them, and eventually buying one is time-consuming and often requires traveling many miles. A professional's reputation is put on the line every time he or she helps to choose a horse.

An *agent's fee* may also include the cost for having the professional be your official representative and negotiator during the actual business transaction. Some professionals add a commission of 10 percent to the price of a horse that they have found for a student. This works fairly well for horses in the $3,000 to $15,000 price range, but it may be inappropriate for horses above or below that range. A flat fee of $300 might be charged for horses under $3,000 and a negotiable percentage may be used for horses above $15,000.

A *finder's fee*, on the other hand, is a seller's way of saying thank you to another professional who has referred a customer to him or her. For instance, if you contact Trainer A for a particular type of horse, and he or she sends you to Trainer B, from whom you end up buying a horse, Trainer B will likely send Trainer A a check for about 1 to 5 percent of the resulting sale price. So the more professionals involved in the sale, the more commissions could be tacked onto the horse's price.

If more than one agent (trainer, instructor, trader) is involved, often the buyer is responsible for one commission and the seller for the other. You will likely write one check to the owner and one to your agent. Talk to the owner of the horse so you both know the actual sale price. This should be common knowledge, and such openness in transactions will help keep agents honest. Always get a bill of sale from the seller that lists the price and is signed by the owner and agent.

If you only want to employ a professional's assistance for specific portions of your search, you should expect to pay customary expenses, including mileage, meals, lodging, and a looker's fee of perhaps $25 to $50 per horse evaluated. If, after six horses at $25 per look plus expenses, the instructor finds you a $6,000 horse, he or she might consider subtracting the $150 previously paid from the $600 commission for finding.

Where to look   Where do you or your agent begin looking for prospective horses? Regularly check bulletin boards of feed stores, tack shops, and stables. Scour local newspapers, shopper's guides, and both the photo ads and classifieds in regional and national horse publications. Let it be known to respected equine professionals in your area that you are looking for a particular type of horse.

Regularly check bulletin boards of feed stores, tack shops, and stables.

Word of mouth is often the best avenue for buying and selling horses. Large farms and stables may have record books that list the horses currently for sale as well as those recently sold. In addition to photos and pedigrees, each entry might include performance history, health and farrier records, and important information on conformation defects, unusual conditions, and vices. If allowed, browse through the records and take notes to help you decide which horses might fit the bill.

THE BUYING PROTOCOL AND THE BUYING PROCEDURE

When you call to inquire about a horse, even though some of these things might be listed in the ad, ask the following questions:

- What is the horse's price?
- What is his age, sex, size?
- Is the horse currently in work?
- Is he currently being shown?
- Is he sound?
- Does he have any bad habits?
- Why are you selling him?
- How long has he been for sale?

If one or more answers are unacceptable to you, thank the seller and tell him or her that you will keep the horse in mind. If the answers to the questions seem reasonable, you have taken a few minutes of the seller's time to determine that the horse is a prospect. Ask when it would be convenient for you to come and take a look at the horse.

Realize that at any time during the horse-buying procedure, if you don't feel a particular horse is for you, you should say so. Thank the seller for telling you about the horse or showing you the horse, but don't waste any more of the seller's or your time.

If you phone ahead to schedule an appointment, most competent sellers will have the requested horses ready for you to view. It is discourteous to arrive for the first visit unannounced and then ask to see everything in the barn. Later on in your relationship with a seller, if you are showing continued interest in a horse, it is all right with many sellers (and advised by many agents) to arrive unannounced so that you can see your prospect in his natural routine.

During your first visit (with or without your agent), perform the buyer exam as outlined in chapter 4. It is not necessary to complete the exam if you find in the first few minutes that the horse is not in contention. If the horse passes your initial conformation and movement assessment, ask to see the horse worked.

Some sellers will allow you to assist in the grooming and saddling of the horse for temperament evaluation. But during the first visit, you should stand back and observe. If you come back a second time, it would be appropriate for you to ask if you could catch, groom and tack the horse, providing you are capable. Also during the second visit, be sure to examine the horse's living quarters. (See chapter 5).

Customarily, a horse will be either longed or ridden for you so that you can see the horse's movement. A trainer can best exhibit a horse's talents and level of training. If, after watching the horse move, you or your instructor don't feel he is suitable, it is more polite to say so than to waste time riding a horse that is not a prospect.

If the horse still looks promising, watch the seller or the horse's regular rider demonstrate the horse's training and way of going. Then either take a test ride (chapter 4) yourself or ask your agent to test the horse.

Before you take the first trial ride on a horse, the seller may ask you to sign a release or disclaimer of liability in case of accident. Although such a waiver may not hold up in court as a legal document, it does outline your risk in specific terms and proves that said risk was pointed out to you by the seller.

The seller is usually equipped to provide you with the appropriate tack to test ride the horse, but often you can use your own saddle, if you have one. Always wear a protective helmet when riding an unfamiliar horse.

Depending on the situation, the trial ride may be a casual familiarization or a more formal lesson with coaching. Advanced maneuvers are best performed by the horse's trainer, not by a prospective buyer. If you are having difficulties re-solving a problem with the horse, the seller has the right to step in and initiate a polite closure of the session. Ending with a positive experience for both you and the horse preserves the horse's training and your safety.

In one way or another a seller gives valuable information about each horse in his barn. If you observe carefully and listen attentively, you can gather interesting facts and draw important conclusions about the manners and personality of the horse you are considering. But don't act like a ruthless detective and skeptic as you examine a horse. If you are inexperienced but have read about all the things that can be wrong with a horse, you might feel you have to cleverly uncover a secret unsoundness to prove you won't be taken advantage of. It is disconcerting for an honest seller to be treated with suspicion and can serve to drive a wedge in future negotiations if things go that far.

It would be inappropriate for you, no matter what your level of experience, to give an analysis of a horse or his training after seeing him once or after riding him for ten or fifteen minutes. You or your instructor would likely alienate a seller by degrading one of his or her horses. Detrimental remarks are unnecessary and in poor taste. Save your comments for when you and your instructor have time to discuss the horse privately, perhaps on the way to look at the next horse.

After you have been in contact with a seller several times over a horse, a relationship begins to develop, and it pays to keep all interactions courteous, positive, and businesslike.

You may wish to try the horse out more extensively. Unfortunately, very few sellers feel comfortable letting a horse go away on trial. The first week for a new horse and rider, especially in a new setting for the horse, can be risky: dangerous for the rider or damaging to the horse's training if he is improperly ridden. When a horse is out on trial, it is difficult or impossible for the seller to show the horse to a backup buyer. The horse is essentially "off the market," so you are asking quite a lot of a seller to let you take a horse on a one- to two-week trial. If you are a student of a respected instructor, however, and your instructor has safe facilities, a seller may let the horse go out on trial to you under your instructor's supervision.

Before a horse goes out on trial, be sure you have in writing an agreement with the seller stating the length of time, the price of the horse, who pays for minor medical costs, feed, and farrier expense (usually the buyer), who pays for major medical emergencies (usually the seller), what happens in the event the horse is permanently injured, and who provides what type of insurance (see chapter 7). If the horse already has a policy, the seller must notify the insurance agent that the horse will be moved, and the agent will need your name and address. You should look at a copy of the insurance policy or make a copy of it. If the horse is not insured, you will need to take out a policy for the trial period, which will cost between $100 and $200. Be sure you have your own liability insurance that covers you in the event the horse injures someone while in your charge during the trial period. The agreement should be signed by both you and the seller and notarized.

If you cannot arrange a trial period but you are fairly certain that you have found *the* horse, then it might be best to put a deposit on him. Some sellers require a pre-purchase agreement (see chapter 6) while you are taking care of the final details (pre-purchase exam), which may require several days to a week or more. During that time, visit the horse and handle him to make very sure that if you buy him he is the horse you want.

After the horse passes the pre-purchase exam, there is other paperwork (chapter 7) to complete.

Chapter Four

Buyer Exam

Conformation should be carefully evaluated whether the horse is a foal, an aged breeding animal, or a performance horse. Conformation has a strong impact on movement, performance, and soundness. While movement is most obvious as motion of the lower limbs, it is an integration of the action of the upper limbs, back, neck—in fact, the whole horse. Therefore, overall conformation must be considered when discussing the athletic potential of a horse. Certain conformation tends to lead to certain types of performance and also to certain kinds of unsoundness. There are no absolutes, however, when it comes to predicting a horse's length of stride, degree of flexion, or directness of travel. Generalizations related to stance, breed, or type are peppered with exceptions.

EVALUATING CONFORMATION AND MOVEMENT

Conformation refers to the physical appearance of a horse as dictated primarily by his bone and muscle structures and by his outline. It is impractical to set a single standard of perfection or to specifically define *ideal* or *normal* conformation because the guidelines depend on the classification, type, breed, and intended use of a horse. A conformation evaluation should always relate to specific function.

When discrepancies are discovered, it is important to differentiate between blemishes and unsoundnesses. *Blemishes* are scars and irregularities that do not affect the serviceability of the horse. *Unsoundnesses* cause a horse to be lame or otherwise unserviceable. Unsoundnesses include lameness caused by such conditions as navicular syndrome, wounds, ringbone, sidebone, spavin, thoroughpin, curb, and bowed tendons as well as miscellaneous conditions such as broken wind, blindness, and retained testicles.

Horses are *classified* as draft (heavy) horses, light horses, or ponies. Classifications are further divided by *type,* according to overall body style, conformation, and the work for which the horse is best suited. Refer to the chart in chapter 2.

A *breed* is a group of horses with common ancestry and usually strong conformational similarities. In most cases, a horse must come from approved breeding stock to be registered with a particular breed. If a horse is not eligible for registration, he is considered a *grade,* or *crossbred,* horse.

Several breeds can have similar makeup and be of the same type. For example, most Quarter Horses, Paint Horses, and Appaloosas are considered stock horse types. Some breeds contain individuals of different types within the breed. American Thoroughbreds can be of the race, hunter, or sport horse type.

Making a Visual Assessment

Develop a specific system for evaluating the horses you are considering. That way, you will have a better means of comparison. Be aware that wildly colored horses and those with dramatic leg markings can cause visual distortions, which could result in inaccurate conclusions. When you examine a horse, be sure it is standing on level ground with weight on all four feet.

Examine the horse in profile

Observe the angle and the manner in which the shoulder attaches to the body.

Begin by looking at a horse from the near side (the horse's left side) in profile and assess overall balance by comparing the forehand to the hindquarters. When viewing the horse in profile, pay attention to the curvature and proportions of the topline. Let your eyes travel from poll to tail and down to the gaskin. Then observe the manner in which the limbs attach to the body. Evaluate hip and shoulder angles.

Step to the front of the horse and evaluate the limbs and hooves for straightness and symmetry. Observe the depth and length of the muscles in the forearm and chest. Evaluate the head, eyes, nostrils, ears, and teeth. Be sure the teeth meet evenly, with no undershot or overshot jaw.

Then step to the off side (the horse's right side) and confirm or modify your evaluation of the balance, topline, and limb angles.

Move to the hindquarter and stand directly behind the tail. Evaluate the straightness and symmetry of the back, croup, point of hip and buttock, and the limbs. Let your eyes run slowly from the poll to the tail, as this is the best vantage point for evaluating back muscling and (provided the horse is standing square) left-to-right symmetry. You may need to elevate your position if you are evaluating a tall horse. The spring of rib is also best observed from the rear view.

Now make another entire circle around the horse, this time stopping at each quadrant to look diagonally across the center of the horse. From your position at the rear of the horse, step to the left hind and look toward the right front. This angle will often reveal abnormalities in the limbs and hooves that were missed

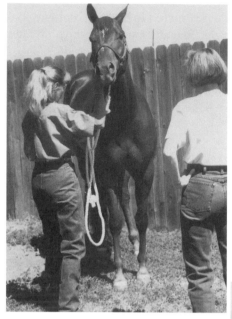

Step to the front of the horse and observe the limbs and hooves for straightness and symmetry.

Move to the hindquarters and stand directly behind the tail.

Check for symmetry of the croup.

during the side, front, and rear examinations. Proceed to the left front and look back toward the right hind. Move to the right front and look toward the left hind. Complete the revolution at the right hind, looking toward the left front.

And finally, step to the near side and take in a view of the whole horse in profile once again.

While you are looking at a horse, it helps if you get an overall sense of the correctness of each of the four functional sections: the head/neck, the forehand, the barrel, and the hindquarters.

Head and neck   The vital senses are located in the head, so it should be correct and functional. Because the neck acts as a lever to help regulate the horse's balance while moving, it should be long and flexible with a slight convex curve to its topline.

Forehand   The front limbs, which support approximately 65 percent of the horse's body weight, must be strong and sound. The majority of lameness is associated with the front limbs.

Barrel   The midsection houses the vital organs, therefore the horse must be adequate in the heart girth and have good spring to the ribs. The back should be well muscled and strong so the horse can carry the weight of the rider and the saddle.

Hindquarters   The rear hand is the source of power and propulsion. The hindquarter muscling should be appropriate for the type, breed, and use. The croup and points of the hip and buttock should be symetrical and the limbs should be straight and sound.

Conformation Components

Balance   A well-balanced horse has a better chance of moving efficiently with less stress. Balance refers to the relationship between the forehand and hindquarters, between the limbs and the trunk of the body, and between the right and the left sides of the horse.

The center of gravity is a theoretical point in the horse's body around which the mass of the horse is equally distributed. At a standstill, the center of gravity is the point of intersection of a vertical line dropped from the highest point of the withers and a line from the point of the shoulder to the point of the buttock. This usually is a spot behind the elbow and about two-thirds the distance down from the topline of the back.

Although the center of gravity remains relatively constant when a well-balanced horse moves, most horses must learn to rebalance their weight (and that of the rider and tack) when ridden. In order to simply pick up a front foot to step forward, the horse must shift his weight rearward. How much the weight must shift to the hindquarters depends on the horse's conformation, the position of the rider, the gait, the degree of collection, and the style of the performance. The more a horse collects, the more he steps under his center of gravity with his hind limbs.

If the forehand is proportionately larger than the hindquarters, especially if it is associated with a downhill topline, the horse's center of gravity tends to be forward. This causes the horse to travel heavy on his front feet, setting the stage for increased concussion, stress, and lameness. When the forehand and hindquarters are balanced and the withers are level with or higher than the level of the croup, the horse's center of gravity is located more rearward. Such a horse can carry more weight with his hindquarters, thus move in balance and exhibit a lighter, freer motion with his forehand than the horse with withers lower than the croup.

When evaluating yearlings, take into consideration the growth spurts that result in a temporarily uneven topline. However, be suspicious of a two year old that shows an extreme downhill configuration. Even if a horse's topline is level, if he has an excessively heavily muscled forehand in comparison to his hindquarters, he is probably going to travel heavy on the forehand and have difficulty moving forward freely.

When evaluating young horses, take growth spurts into consideration. This twelve-month-old Quarter Horse filly is lower in the withers.

The same filly as in the previous photograph (and in photographs on pages 55, 56, and 58) at twenty-four months. Notice how the pastern angles and topline have moderated.

A balanced horse has approximately equal *lower limb* (front) length and depth of body. The lower limb length (chest floor to the ground) should be equal to the distance from the chest floor to the top of the withers. Proportionately shorter lower limbs are associated with a choppy stride.

The horse's *height* or *overall limb length* (point of withers to ground) should approximate the length of the horse's body (the point of the shoulder to the point of buttock). A horse with a body a great deal longer than its height often experiences difficulty in synchronization and coordination of movement. A horse with limbs proportionately longer than the body may be predisposed to forging, overreaching and other gait defects.

When viewing a horse overall, the right side of the horse should be symmetric to the left side.

Proportions and curvature of the topline The ratio of the topline's components, the curvature of the topline, the strength of loin, the sharpness of withers, the slope to the croup, and the length of the underline in relation to the length of back all affect a horse's movement.

The neck is measured from the poll to the highest point of the withers. The back measurement is taken from the withers to the center of the loin, located above the last rib and in front of the pelvis. The hip length is measured from the

P = poll
W = highest point
    of withers
L = loin
B = point of buttock
S = point of shoulder
C = center of gravity
U = underline
G = ground
WU = depth of body
UG = lower limb
    length
WG = height and over-
    all limb length
SB = length of body
PW = length of neck
WL = length of back
LB = length of hip

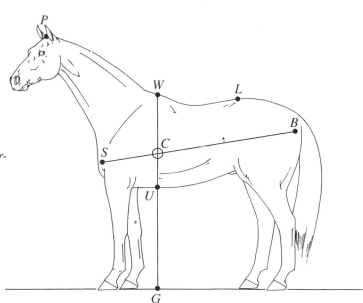

Center of gravity and proportions. From Hill and Klimesh, Maximum Hoof Power.

center of the loin to the point of buttock. Notice that the point of hip is located directly below the center of the loin. Commonly the hip length is the distance between the point of hip and the point of buttock.

A neck that is shorter than the back tends to decrease a horse's overall flexibility and balance. Be sure to look at the neck from both sides, because the mane side often appears shorter than the non-mane side. A back that is a great deal longer than the neck tends to hollow. A very short hip, in relation to the neck or back, is associated with lack of propulsion and often a downhill configuration. A rule of thumb is that the neck should be greater than or equal to the back and that the hip should be at least two-thirds the length of the back.

The neck should have a graceful shape that rises up out of the withers, not dip downward in front of the withers. The upward curve to the neck should be more pronounced in a dressage prospect than in a hunter or western prospect. The shape of the neck is determined by the S shape formed by the seven cervical vertebrae. A longer, flatter (more horizontal) configuration to the upper vertebrae results in a smoother attachment at the poll (as if the neck is _behind_ the skull, or the head is attached on the end of a flexible balancing arm) and results in a cleaner, more supple throatlatch. If the upper vertebrae form a short, diagonal line to the skull, it is associated with an abrupt attachment (as if the neck attaches _below_ the skull, or the head is stuck on top of the neck), resulting in a thick throatlatch, lack of flexibility, and possibly a hammerhead.

The curve to the lower neck vertebrae should be short and shallow and attach relatively high on the horse's chest. The thickest point in the neck is at the base of the lower curve. Ewe-necked horses often have necks that have an undesirable long, deep lower curve and attach low to the chest. The attachment of the neck to the shoulder should be smooth, without an abnormal dip in front of the shoulder blade.

The upper neck length (poll to withers) should be at least twice the lower neck length (throatlatch to chest). This is dictated to a large degree by the slope of the shoulder. A horse with a very steep shoulder has an undesirable ratio (approaching 1:1) between the upper neck length and lower neck length. The more sloping the shoulder, the longer the neck's top line becomes and the shorter the neck's underline. The muscling of the topline of the neck should be more developed than the muscling of the underside of the neck. A thick underside to the neck is associated with a horse that braces against the bit and hollows the neck's topline.

The back should look like it has a natural place for a saddle, beginning with prominent withers that are located above or slightly behind (but not exaggeratedly in front of) the heart girth. The heart girth is the circumference of the barrel just behind the front limbs. The withers should gradually blend into the back, ideally ending just in front of the midpoint of the back. The withers provide a place for the neck muscles and ligamentum nuchae to anchor, and they should attach at the highest point of the withers; there should not be a dip in front of or behind the withers.

The withers also act as a fulcrum. As a horse lowers and extends its neck, the back rises. Low, mutton withers limit a horse's ability to raise his back. A horse with a well-sloped shoulder usually has correctly placed withers. The heart girth should be deep, indicating adequate room for the heart and lungs.

The muscles that run alongside the spine should be flat and strong rather than sloped or weak. The back muscles must help counteract the gravitational pull from the weight of the horse's intestines as well as support the rider's weight. The line of the back should be flat or level, not hollow (dipped or concave) or roached (bowed up or convex). A hollow back is associated with weakness and a roached back with stiffness.

The loin is located along the lumbar vertebrae from the last rib-bearing (dorsal) vertebrae to the lumbosacral joint. The loin should be well muscled and relatively short. Horses termed "long-backed" often have an acceptable back length but a long, weak loin. A horse with a weak and/or long loin and loose coupling tends to have a hollow back. (The coupling is the area behind the last rib and in front of a vertical line dropped from the point of hip.) A horse that chronically hollows its back may be predisposed to back problems.

The loin and the coupling are what transfer the motion of the hindquarters up through the back and forward to the forehand, so they must be strong and well connected. A short, heavily muscled loin has great potential strength, power, and durability, yet could lack the flexibility that a more moderately muscled loin may have. Loin muscling (best viewed from the top) should appear springy and resilient, not stiff and cramped or weak and saggy. A lumpy appearance in the loin area may indicate partial dislocations of the vertebrae.

The croup is measured from the lumbosacral joint (approximately indicated by the peak above and slightly behind the points of hip) to the tail head. The croup should be fairly long, as this is associated with a good length to the hip and a desirable, forward-placed lumbosacral joint. The slope to the croup will depend on the breed and use. Quarter Horses and Thoroughbreds traditionally have round croups; Arabians and warmbloods have flat croups.

The topline should be "short" relative to the underline. Such a combination indicates strength plus desirable length of stride.

Head　The head should be functionally sound. The brain coordinates the horse's movements, so adequate cranial space is necessary. The length from the base of the ear to the eye should be at least one-third the distance from ear to nostril. The width between the eyes should be a similar distance as that from the base of the ear to the eye. A wide poll with ears far apart is associated with the atlas connecting behind the skull rather than below it. A wide open throatlatch allows proper breathing during flexion; a narrow throatlatch is often associated with a ewe-neck attachment. Eyes set off to the side of the head allow the horse to have a panoramic view. The eye should be prominent without bulging. Prominence refers to the bony eye socket, not a protruding eyeball. The expression of the eye should indicate a quiet, tractable temperament.

The muzzle can be trim, but if it is too small, the nostrils may be pinched and there may be inadequate space for the incisors, resulting in dental misalignments. The incisors should meet evenly, with no overhang of the upper incisors (parrot mouth) or jutting out of the lower incisors (monkey mouth). The width of the cheek bones indicates the space for molars; adequate room is required for the sideways grinding of food. The shape of the nasal bone and forehead is largely a matter of breed and personal preference.

Quality   Quality is depicted by "flat" bone (indicated by the cannon bone), clean joints, sharply defined (refined) features, smooth muscling, overall blending of parts, and a fine, smooth hair coat. "Flat" bone is a misnomer, because the cannon bone is round. "Flat" actually refers to well-defined tendons that stand out cleanly behind the cannon bone and give the impression the bone is flat.

Substance   This refers to thickness, depth, and breadth of bone, muscle, and other tissues. Muscle substance is described by type of muscle, thickness of muscle, length of muscles, and position of attachment. Other substance factors include weight of the horse, height of the horse, size of the hooves, depth of the heart girth and flank, and spring of rib.

Best viewed from the rear, spring of rib refers to the curve of the ribs; a flat-ribbed horse may have inadequate heart and lung space. Besides providing room for the heart, lungs, and digestive tract, a well-sprung rib cage provides a natural, comfortable place for a rider's legs. A slab-sided horse with a shallow heart girth is difficult to sit properly; an extremely wide-barreled horse can be stressful to the rider's pelvis and legs.

The rear view allows you to evaluate spring of rib and further examine the hind limbs.

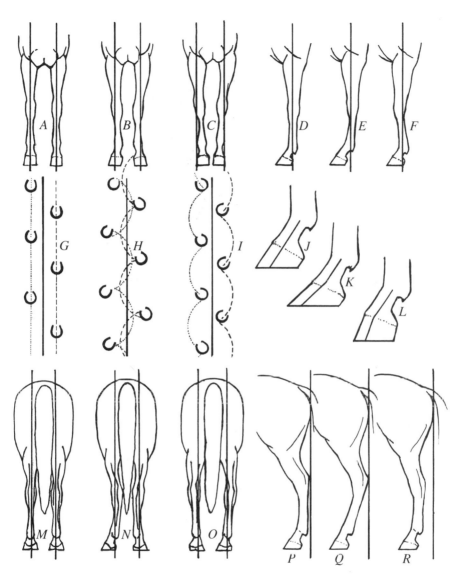

Leg conformation and travel. From Hill, From the Center of the Ring.

A = correct
B = toed-out
C = toed-in
D = correct
E = calf knee
F = buck knee
G = straight travel
H = winging in
I = paddling

J = desirable hoof alignment
K = broken back axis
L = broken forward axis
M = correct
N = cow-hocked, toed-out
O = bow-legged, toed-in
P = correct
Q = sickle hocked
R = post legged

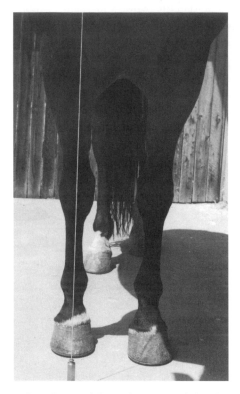

A line dropped from the point of shoulder to the ground should bisect the limb and hoof.

Substance of bone indicates adequacy of the ratio of the bone to the horse's body weight. Bone measurement is taken on an adult horse around the circumference of the cannon bone just below the knee. For riding horses, an adequate ratio is approximately .7 inches of bone for every 100 pounds of body weight. Using that thumb rule, a 1,200-pound horse should have approximately an 8.4-inch-circumference cannon bone for his weight to be adequately supported.

Correctness of angles and structures   The correct alignment of the skeletal components provides the framework for muscular attachments. The length and slope to the shoulder, arm, forearm, croup, hip, stifle, and pasterns should be moderate and work well together. There should be a straight alignment of bones and large clean joints when viewed from front and rear.

Forelimbs   Both forelimbs should appear to be of equal length and size and to bear equal weight. A line dropped from the point of the shoulder to the ground should bisect the limb. The toes should point forward and the feet should be as far apart on the ground as the limbs are at their origin in the chest. The shoulder should be well-muscled without being heavy and coarse.

The muscles running along the inside and outside of the forearm should go all the way to the knee, ending in a gradual taper, rather than ending abruptly a few inches above the knee. It is generally felt that this will allow the horse to use its front limbs in a smooth-sweeping, forward motion. The pectoral muscles at the horse's chest floor (an inverted V) should also reach far down onto the limb. These and the forearm muscles help a horse move its limbs laterally and medially as well as to elevate the forehand.

Front limbs, when viewed from the side should exhibit a composite of moderate angles, so that shock absorption will be efficient. The shoulder angle is measured along the spine of the scapula from the point of the shoulder to the point of the withers. The shorter and straighter the shoulder, the shorter and quicker the stride and the more stress and concussion transmitted to the limb. Also important is the angle the shoulder makes with the arm (which should be at least 90 degrees) and the angle of the pastern.

The length of the humerus (point of shoulder to the point of elbow) affects stride length. A long humerus is associated with a long reaching stride and good lateral ability; a short humerus, with a short choppy stride and poor lateral ability. The steeper the angle of the humerus, generally the higher the action; the more toward horizontal, the lower the action.

To evaluate the medial-lateral slope of the humerus from the front, find the left point of shoulder and (a spot in front of) the left point of elbow. Do the same on the right side. Connect the four points. If the resulting box is square, the humerus lies in an ideal position for straight lower limbs and straight travel. If the bottom of the box is wider, the horse may toe in and travel with loose elbows and paddle. If the bottom of the box is narrower, the horse will likely toe out, have tight elbows, and wing in.

The way the shoulder blade and arm (humerus) are conformed and attach to the chest dictate, to a large degree, the alignment of the lower limbs. Whether the toes point in or out is often a result of upper limb structures. That is why it is dangerous in many cases to attempt to alter a limb's structure and alignment through radical hoof adjustments. When assessing the lower limbs, be sure the horse is standing square.

The knees should be large and clean, not small and puffy. The bone column should be functionally straight and sound, not buck-kneed (over at the knee) or calf-kneed (back at the knee). The calf-kneed horse suffers strain at the back of the knee and concussion at the front of the knee, which can result in carpal chips and other problems. The buck-kneed horse is unstable, as the knees shake and are on the verge of buckling forward.

The flexor tendons running behind the cannon bone should be even and straight, not pinched in (tied in) at the back of the knee or lumpy (indicating possible bowed tendon) anywhere from the knee to the fetlock.

Normal front pastern angles range from 53 to 58 degrees. Exceptionally long, sloping pasterns can result in tendon strain, bowed tendon, and damaged

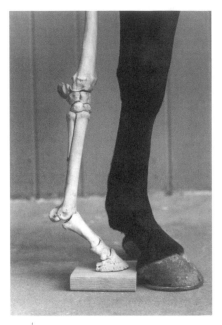

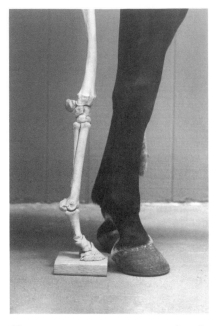

Viewing the limb from the side gives an idea of the angle of the pastern and possible problems. This horse's sloping pasterns deliver a springy ride but could result in tendon problems in the future.

Short, steep pasterns are associated with a choppy stride and concussion-related problems.

Take a good look at the front legs, because you will feel their effects as you ride.

proximal sesamoids. Short, upright pasterns deliver greater concussive stresses to fetlock and pastern joints, which may result in osselets, ringbone, and possibly navicular syndrome. Fetlock joints should be large enough to allow free movement, but they should be devoid of any puffiness. The hoof should be appropriate for the size of the horse, well shaped and symetrical, with high-quality hoof horn, adequate height and width of heel, and a concave sole. The hoof angle should be the same as the pastern angle, making a smooth continuous line. (*See Maximum Hoof Power* in the appendix for more information on hoof conformation and management.)

Hind limbs The bone structure and muscling of the hind limbs should be appropriate for the intended use. Endurance horses are characterized by longer, flatter muscles; stock horses by shorter, thicker muscles; all-around horses by moderate muscles.

When viewed from the side, hind limbs should exhibit a composite of moderate angles, so that shock absorption will be efficient. A line from the point of buttock to the ground should touch the hock and end slightly behind the bulbs of the heels. A hind limb in front of this line is often sickle-hocked; a hind limb behind this line is often post-legged or camped out.

The hoof should be appropriate for the size of the horse, as this one is.

The hindquarter should be symmetric and well connected to the barrel and the lower limb. The gluteals should tie well forward into the back. The hamstrings should tie down low into the Achilles tendon of the hock.

The relationship of the length of the bones, the angles of the joints, and the overall height of the hind limbs will dictate the type of action and the amount of power produced. The length and slope to the pelvis is measured from the point of hip to the point of buttock and is generally closely related to the length and slope of the croup. A flat, level croup is associated with hind limb action that occurs *behind* the hindquarters rather than underneath it. A goose rump is a very steep croup that places the hind limbs so far under the horse's belly that structural problems may occur due to the over-angulation.

A short femur is associated with the short, rapid stride characteristic of a sprinter. A long femur results in a stride with more reach. High hocks are associated with snappy hock action and a difficulty getting the hocks under the body. Low hocks tend to have a smoother hock action, and the horse usually has an easier time getting the hocks under the body. The gaskin length (stifle to hock) should be shorter than the femur length (buttock to stifle). A gaskin longer than the femur tends to be associated with cow hocks and sickle hocks.

Hind limbs with open angles (a "straighter" hind limb when viewed from the side) have a shorter overall limb length and produce efficient movement suitable for hunters or race horses. Hind limbs with more closed joints (more angulation to the joints of the hind limb) have a longer overall limb length and produce a more vertical, folding action necessary for the collection characteristic of a high-level dressage horse. If the overall limb length is too long, however, it can be associated with either camped-out or sickle-hocked conformation. No matter what the hind limb conformation is at rest, however, it is the way it connects to the loin and operates in motion that is most important.

From the rear, both hind limbs should appear symmetric, to be of the same length and to bear equal weight. A left-to-right symmetry should be evident between the peaks of the croup, the points of the hip, the points of the buttock, and the midline position of the tail. The widest point of the hindquarters should be the width between the stifles. A line dropped from the point of the buttock to the ground will essentially bisect the limb, but hind limbs are not designed to point absolutely straight forward. It is necessary and normal for the stifles to point slightly outward in order to clear the horse's belly. This causes the points of the hocks to face slightly inward and the toes to point outward to the same degree. The rounder the belly and/or the shorter the loin and coupling, the more the stifles must point out so the more the points of the hocks will appear to point inward. The more slab-sided and/or longer coupled a horse, the more straight ahead the stifles and hocks can point. When the cannon bone faces outward, the horse is often cow-hocked; when cannons face inward, bowlegged.

Soundness problems can occur when the hocks point absolutely straight ahead and the hooves toe out; *then* there is stress on the hock and fetlock joints. The

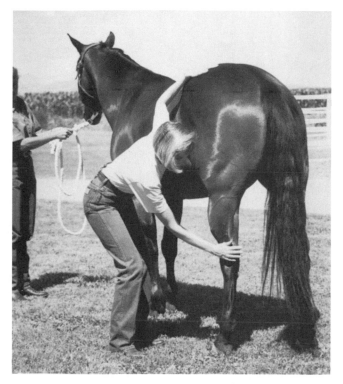

Hocks should be devoid of puffiness and bony enlargements.

hind feet should be as far apart on the ground as the limbs are at their origin in the hip. Normal hind pastern angles range from 55 to 60 degrees.

EVALUATING POTENTIAL OF YOUNG HORSES

Good character and desirable performance are a result of both inherited and acquired factors, but a top-notch horse will more likely emerge from a horse that possesses special traits from birth. If you are purchasing a young horse, observe it as it interacts in a natural setting with other horses and as it responds to simple handling tests. It will be most useful if you compare the reactions of several horses of the same age.

Attitude, temperament, and mental powers Intelligence plus adaptability equals trainability. To begin evaluating a young horse's mental set, note his sense of independence. An insecure horse has a much more difficult time reaching his full performance potential. Horses high in the pecking order in a herd may initially be more difficult to train but may later show more brilliance during performance. A horse that is low in the hierarchy might be easy to dominate but will

Observe suckling foals in a natural setting.

need constant reward in order to develop and maintain his self-confidence. For demanding sports such as dressage, hunting, and eventing, it is often more effective to teach willing cooperation to an aggressive horse than it is to develop boldness in a meek individual. In the same light, a ranch horse needs to be comfortable dominating cattle and other horses and doing his work in all kinds of weather and footing, so a ranch horse must also be a confident individual.

Bonding between horses in herds (or stables) can present a problem. A horse with a low independence aptitude is often more concerned with the location of his stable mate than with his rider's cues or even, at times, with his own safety. Youngsters that have been weaned without trauma, that have enjoyed the companionship of a variety of herd mates, and that have been handled as individuals from birth tend to be curious and adventuresome. Try leading a yearling away from his herd mates or, if this is not possible, observe him in a safe pen separate from the others. You can expect a few whinnies initially, but if the noise persists or builds to a frenzy, the horse lacks confidence. The insecure horse will be oblivious to attempts made by you or the horse's owner to get his attention. If you enter his pen, he will either turn his rump toward you or ignore you as he wheels around the pen. The insecure horse often does not pay attention to the dangers and the limits of his confines. Some young horses crash into fences and heavy pens in an attempt to rejoin their herd mates.

The foal that is curious about humans generally accepts the interactions of training more willingly than the foal that turns away.

A horse with a high degree of self-confidence is usually quite independent. He notices his separation from other horses, but chooses to investigate his new surroundings. The confident horse remains alert to things going on around him. If you or his owner were to enter his pen, he would acknowledge your presence by turning and facing you. The well-socialized horse will walk toward you.

A confident horse tends to have a high degree of self-preservation, that is, the inherent sense to take care of himself and keep himself from harm. A young horse with a low self-preservation aptitude may stumble over things on the ground out of carelessness, might panic through a fence, or might have trouble locating feed and water areas when he is put in new facilities. Self-preservation is a combination of confidence, alertness, and "horse sense." It is desirable for a horse to be alert to the point that he notices things but does not fear them or overreact to them. It is part of the horse's nature to be wary of unusual circumstances, yet you don't want a young horse that is suspicious of everything. On the other hand, you don't want a horse that is a "deadhead," one that seems uninterested in anything going on.

To assess self-preservation, prepare a test pen with safe fencing. Place a few poles on the ground in a random fashion but where the horse must cross them; put a half-full bucket of water in the middle of the pen; lay an empty paper feed sack on the ground with a handful of grain on it. Put the horse in the pen and note his reactions. The secure horse with low self-preservation might stumble over the rails as if they posed no threat, might paw the bucket and tip it over, will probably give little notice to the feed sack by shuffling past it or pawing it and wasting the grain. The insecure horse with low self-preservation might trot wildly around the pen and shy at the various objects or stand snorting in a corner with no intentions of inspecting anything. The secure horse with high self-preservation might pause as he enters the pen and survey the overall scene. He might look down and sniff each rail as he carefully steps over, sniff the water in the pail without touching the sides of the bucket, and inspect the sack by smelling and then would probably eat the grain. Then he might stand calmly in a location that allows him to keep an eye on all of the new objects.

Horses vary greatly in their tolerance for stress. Positive experiences can increase a horse's stress tolerance but in spite of good training and conditioning, some horses will always be "thin-skinned" and break down easily when their low sensory threshold is reached. To measure a horse's ability to sort out harmful stress and to see how he reacts to stress, ask the owner to clap her hands near the horse's pen. Ask her if you can take off your jacket and shake the dust off it. Is the horse frightened or merely attentive to these things?

Some horses are better than others in adapting to the requirements and pressures of domestication. Certain horses don't accept confinement. A horse that has

A well-socialized foal respects but does not fear humans.

Approach a group of horses in a pen and note which ones face you, which ones ignore you, and which ones move away.

lived on pasture all of his life might find it hard to adapt to a new, smaller environment. Conversely, some horses that have been stalled from birth are not comfortable living in a pasture and become "gate potatoes," standing or pacing at a gate, perhaps whinnying for attention. A broad base of experience early in a horse's life helps him feel comfortable in a variety of circumstances. To gauge a horse's ability to adapt, ask if a normally pastured horse could be put in a stall (or a stalled horse in a pasture) and watch the horse's behavior initially and over the next several days if possible. Does the horse immediately locate the source for food and water? Does he inspect the boundaries? Does he develop a defecation pattern, or does he nervously spread manure everywhere? Does he show signs of discomfort and distress by pawing, pacing, weaving, cribbing, or wood chewing? Does he stand at the pasture gate the majority of the time? How long does it take the horse to develop his new daily routines?

A horse that has been properly socialized with man has interest in and respect for humans but does not fear them. Some foals and yearlings are "all horse" and are somewhat aloof, while others seem to prefer human interaction and companionship to that of their own species. Approach a group of horses in a pen. Staying the critical distance from them so that they settle, note which ones face you with alert ears and which ones turn and move away or huddle with their rumps toward you. Turning a rump toward a human can indicate either fear or a lack of respect. Close the distance between you and the herd. Do those facing you turn and move away, hold their ground, or begin to step toward you? Watch the ears and head positions of the horses that have their rumps toward you. Which would be more likely to stand their ground and kick at an intruder, and which would rather flee?

If you have the opportunity to lead a young horse, lead him on a slack line at a walk, trot, and halt. If the horse crowds you and pushes in front of you, stepping on your toes, he likely lacks respect. If he swings to face you on a taut line, he could be fearful or arrogant. I've found the best kind of horse to train is the one that is alert and slightly wary of the handler's moves.

An honest horse makes his intentions clear and keeps no secrets from his handler. A testy horse seems as if he has learned a lesson, but regularly regresses, requiring frequent review and retraining. Dishonest horses are often very devious. They know what they should and should not do. They won't try something naughty if they know they will be caught. But when the handler is at a disadvantage, the dishonest horse will take the opportunity to misbehave.

To assess honesty, review something the horse has supposedly been taught to do well, such as unhaltering and turning loose. Be casual in your method, such as not retaining control of the horse with your arms or the lead rope as you unhalter. This is "baiting" the horse to do something wrong. The dishonest horse will sense

This alert, cooperative yearling filly (the weanling in the photographs on pages 55 and 58) learns a new lesson in a short period of time.

This three-month-old Trakehner/Quarter Horse filly shows excellent balance and proportion, like a scaled-down version of an adult horse.

the opportunity and may pull and wheel away prematurely. The honest horse will wait until your body language or voice tells him he can step away.

The alert, cooperative horse learns a new lesson in a relatively short period of time. The tuned-out, sullen, or belligerent horse may require many lessons and frequent reviews. Ask the horse's owner to perform a simple exercise with the horse that he has not yet been taught, such as moving over while tied. The sensitive, alert horse often will perform this lesson correctly the first time from light finger pressure, provided he has been set up in the proper position to comply with the trainer's aids. Other horses may resist strongly (lock up) or swing into the handler. How many attempts are necessary before the horse understands what is being asked of him? Once the horse learns what is being asked of him, does he anticipate by moving quickly away as soon as a person approaches him? The best kind of horse to work with is one that learns quickly, requires minimal cuing, and responds to each cue with a separate, appropriate reaction and without anticipation.

Conformation and athletic ability   A young horse's conformation should be evaluated as outlined in chapter 4. However, young horses often do not exhibit desirable balance and proportions, even though they will as adults. Frequently horses under one year of age will stand with hips higher than the withers. Two

Newborn foals, such as this week-old Trakehner/Quarter Horse filly, appear to have very long legs and long pasterns.

The straight pasterns on this two-and-a-half-month-old Quarter Horse filly moderated by the time she was a yearling. (See page 40.)

A two-week-old Trakehner/Quarter Horse filly shows the typical short neck of a young foal. By ten months of age, the neck was long, elegant, and shapely.

year olds that continue to display this downhill configuration should be suspected of retaining it as adults. Newborn foals often appear to have rounded foreheads, short necks, long, sloping shoulders, and long, rubbery pasterns. By weaning time,

Watch a young horse free on pasture to see his tendencies. This three-month-old Selle Français/Quarter Horse colt is a natural conformation prospect.

these factors usually moderate somewhat. In fact, in many cases foals two to twelve months of age will tend to have straighter pasterns than they will as adults. A yearling usually appears long and lean because his frame has increased in height and length but his muscles haven't developed yet. By the time a horse is two years old, you should have a pretty good idea of his balance, proportions, and angles as an adult.

Besides conformation, other physical traits should be considered when purchasing a young horse. Observing young horses at play in a pasture can separate those with the movement for dressage from those that look like naturals for jumping; those with gaits of a Western Pleasure horse from those that have the moves of a reining horse.

The proprioceptive sense allows a horse to rely on transmissions from his nerves and muscles to help him negotiate an obstacle rather than relying entirely on his sight. This is essential for hunter/jumpers, eventers, and trail horses. The simplest way to test a horse's proprioceptive sense is to lead him over several ground rails. They can be irregularly spaced to see if he can "pick" his way through, or the poles can be set specific distances from each other to accommodate the young horse's length of stride.

Assess the foal's coordination, flexibility, and balance. This foal shows natural hindquarter strength and forehand lightness

Young hunter/jumper or trail prospects can also be led or longed over ground rails or cavalletti on the lowest setting. Starting with the rails approximately five feet apart, familiarize the youngster by leading at the walk, and if appropriate, at the trot. Compare the first, second, and third attempts. If the horse maintained composure through all three gos, he's a jewel. I feel it is usually less desirable if a horse does well the first time but his subsequent attempts deteriorate than it is if he lightly taps a rail on the first pass but goes clean after that.

Coordination is closely coupled to the proprioceptive sense. A horse is well coordinated if his body functions harmoniously when performing complex movements. Free-jumping or longeing a long two-year-old over a small course can be very enlightening. Natural talent and balance will show up as the horse goes over a fence the first time. Subsequent attempts might show that the horse is interested in improving his performance or that he is getting careless or bored.

The flexibility of a horse's spine is especially important for dressage, jumping, and reining. A naturally stiff horse can experience pain and resist when he is required to bend. A yearling or two-year-old should be able to arc his head around to each shoulder and hold it there momentarily without distress and without moving his hindquarters. Foals are usually too short-necked and compact to do this. Holding the young horse along a solid fence and trying this on each side will reveal any tendencies of muscular resistance. Watch the way young horses change leads as they play in a pasture. The natural lead changer is usually flexible on both sides of his body as well as coordinated.

A sensitive horse is more receptive to cues. Individuals with large eyes and nostrils and keen hearing perceive more subtle distinctions in their trainer's cues. Nerve endings on the thin-skinned, sensitive horse are close to the surface and readily receive stimuli from the rider's aids. If you are experienced, you may want a very sensitive horse. However, if you are looking for a first-time training project, you might want a horse that is a little "thicker skinned." Approach a group of horses in a pasture. Which one is the first to hear you as you approach? With a horse haltered and tied or held, exert pressure with your thumb and index finger on the horse's tendon just above the fetlock. How much of a pinch was necessary to get the horse to pick up his hoof? Examine the horse's skin on its head and neck. Does it appear to be thin and pliable, with blood vessels noticeable just under the skin, or is the skin thick and tough? Look at the horse's tongue. Is it pink, soft, and glistening or pasty and meaty looking? Inspect the interdental space (the area between the incisors and the molars). Is the jawbone narrow or wide? Is the skin covering it thin or thick?

The young horse's natural balance can be evaluated by trailer loading and free longeing. As a horse loads in a trailer, he experiences a weight shift to his hindquarters and then to his forehand. This should happen smoothly and without exaggerated head and neck movements. When a horse is longed, he should travel in a smooth arc in both directions. If a horse moves stiffly or awkwardly in one direction, he is not naturally balanced. Horses that routinely take the wrong lead or are disunited (one lead in front, the other lead behind) when cantering in a 20-meter (66-foot) circle will have lateral balance and flexibility problems that will need to be worked out in early training.

Joints and tendons need to be elastic yet tough for any athletic performance. Although long, sloping pasterns may provide a more comfortable ride in some cases, they are usually associated with weak joints and (bowed) tendons. Watch a young prospect play in a deep sand pen, in a hard-surfaced paddock, or in a pasture with uneven terrain. In each case, watch the flexion and extension of the joints and the horse's overall freedom of movement.

Physical relaxation is necessary for maximum athletic achievement. A horse that does not release tension is working against himself during performance. Muscles are essentially involved in a give-and-take situation as they contract and relax. If a horse is a great muscle contractor but a poor muscle relaxer, the level of tension in his muscle builds during the work. Similarly, horses must breathe regularly throughout a workout and need to be relaxed in order to establish a desirable breathing rhythm. Watch a young horse in training on the longe line when he is asked to collect himself or extend; look for signs of tension when there is pressure exerted on the bit when sidereins are being used or during ground driving.

Have the horse led directly away from you.

Have the horse led directly toward you.

EVALUATING MOVEMENT

Evaluation of movement and performance requires a certain base of knowledge and a "good eye." To assist in the development of your eye, study horse performances on video using stop action, single frame advance, and slow motion features. If you are inexperienced, view the tapes with your riding instructor or another experienced professional and ask him or her what they see so you can develop your ability to "see" rather than just "look." Take your mentor along when you are looking at prospective horses to buy.

Movement Evaluation Process

If you don't get a satisfactory view at any one of these steps, ask the handler to repeat that part of the process.

1. Have the horse led (on a loose lead so as not to restrict head movement) at a walk directly away from you and then toward you so you get a clear view of how the horse's legs move in relation to each other as well as watch the symmetry of hip movement. If one hip drops or hikes noticeably, beware. This test should be performed on a firm surface so you can see and hear the horse's footfall. Hard ground will reveal joint or skeletal problems. Watch for head bobbing, which indicates lameness.

2. Have the horse trotted toward and away from you on a firm surface.

3. Have the horse walked in a straight line and view the horse about twenty feet from the side to assess head movement, breakover, toe-dragging, stride length (over-tracking), use of shoulder and hip, and manner the hoof is landing (flat is ideal).

4. Have the horse trotted in a straight line and view the horse from the side. Also listen to the cadence of the footfall to be sure it is even.

5. Have the horse longed in soft footing at a walk, trot, and canter. This will uncover any soft tissue problems such as muscles, tendons, or ligaments.

6. Have the horse ridden in normal arena footing.

7. Have the horse ridden over uneven ground or cross-country.

8. Ride the horse yourself (see Test Ride in chapter 5).

Videotaping the performance of a prospective horse is a way to allow you to study a horse in detail later with or without your instructor. The films can provide you with a valuable visual analysis of gait, movement abnormalities, and overall way of going.

Before you can really make a knowledgeable assessment of what you are seeing, be sure you have a good understanding of the gaits, the phases of the stride, and general movement concepts (see sidebars).

THE NATURAL GAITS

The *walk* is a four-beat gait that should have a very even rhythm as the feet land and take off in the following sequence: left hind, left front, right hind, right front. A horse that is rushing at the walk might either jig or prance (impure "gaits" comprised of half walking, half trotting) or he might develop a pacey walk. The *pace* is a two-beat lateral gait where the two right limbs rise and land alternately with the two left limbs. Although the pace is a natural gait for some Standardbred horses and other breeds, a pacey walk is considered an impure gait for most riding horses because the even, four-beat pattern of the walk has been broken. At a normal walk, the horse's hind foot should at least step onto the heel of the forefoot print on the same side.

The *trot* is a two-beat diagonal gait. Traditionally, the trot refers to an English gait with moderate to great impulsion. The (western) jog is a shorter-strided trot with less impulsion. The right front and left hind rise and fall together alternately with the diagonal pair left front and right hind. Often the trot is a horse's steadiest and most rhythmic gait. If a horse is jogged too slow, the gait becomes impure as the diagonal pairs break and the horse essentially jogs behind and walks in front. At a normal trot, the hind feet should at least cover the prints of the front feet.

The *canter* or *lope* is a three-beat gait with the following sequence: one hind limb, then the other hind limb and the diagonal forelimb, and finally the remaining forelimb. If a horse is on the right lead, the initiating hind (sometimes referred to as the driving hind) will be the left hind, the diagonal pair will be the right hind (sometimes referred to as the supporting hind) and the left front, and the final beat will occur when the leading foreleg, the right front, lands. Then there is a moment of suspension as the horse gathers his limbs underneath himself to get organized for the next cycle. (A change of lead should occur during the moment of suspension so that the horse can change front and hind simultaneously.) When observing a horse on the right lead from the side, you can observe that the right limbs reach farther forward than the left limbs. When a horse is loped too slow, it gives rise to a four-beat gait where the diagonal pair has broken and each limb lands separately. The four-beat lope is an impure gait and undesirable.

The *gallop* or *run* is a four-beat, accelerated variation of the canter. With increased impulsion and length of stride, the diagonal pair breaks, resulting in four beats at speed. The footfall sequence of a right lead gallop is left hind, right hind, left front, and right front. As in canter, the right limbs will reach farther forward than the left limbs when the horse is in the right lead. There is a more marked suspension at the gallop than the canter.

The *back*, performed in its correct form, is a two-beat diagonal gait in reverse. The left hind and right front are lifted and placed down together, alternating with the right hind and left front.

THE PHASES OF A STRIDE

The phases of a horse's stride are landing, loading, stance, breakover, and swing.

Landing　The hoof touches the ground, the limb begins to receive the impact of the body's weight.

Loading　The body moves forward and the horse's center of gravity passes over the hoof. Usually this is when the fetlock descends to its lowest point, sometimes resulting in an almost horizontal pastern. The cannon is vertical.

Stance　The fetlock rises to a configuration comparable to the horse's stance at rest. The transition between the loading phase and the stance phase is very stressful to the internal structures of the hoof and lower limb. The horse's center of gravity moves ahead of the hoof. The flexor muscles and tendons lift the weight of the horse (and rider) and the fetlock begins to move upward. The pastern straightens and the limb begins pushing up off the ground.

Breakover　The hoof prepares to leave the ground. This phase starts when the heels lift and the hoof begins to pivot at the toe. At that moment, the knee (or hock) relaxes and begins to flex. Breakover is measured from the time the heels lift to the time the toe leaves the ground. The deep digital flexor tendon (assisted by the suspensory ligament) is still stretched just prior to the beginning of breakover to counteract the downward pressure of the weight of the horse's body.

Swing　The limb moves through the air and straightens out in preparation for landing.

TERMS ASSOCIATED WITH MOVEMENT

Action　The style of the movement, including joint flexion, stride length, and suspension; usually viewed from the side.

Asymmetry　A difference between two body parts or an alteration in the synchronization of a gait; when a horse is performing asymmetrically, he is often said to be "off."

Balance　The harmonious, precise, coordinated form of a horse's movement as reflected by equal distribution of weight from left to right and an appropriate amount of weight carried by the hindquarters.

Breakover　The moment between the stance and swing phases as the heel lifts and the hoof pivots over the toe.

Cadence　*See* Rhythm.

Collection   A shortening of stride within a gait, without a decrease in tempo; brought about by a shift of the center of gravity rearward; usually accompanied by an overall body elevation and an increase in joint flexion.

Directness   Trueness of travel, the straightness of the line in which the hoof (limb) is carried forward.

Evenness   Balance, symmetry, and synchronization of the steps within a gait in terms of weight-bearing and timing.

Extension   A lengthening of stride within a gait, without an increase in tempo, brought about by a driving force from behind and a reaching in front; usually accompanied by a horizontal floating called *suspension.*

Gait   An orderly footfall pattern such as the walk, trot, canter.

Height   The degree of elevation of arc of the stride, viewed from the side.

Impulsion   Thrust, the manner in which the horse's weight is settled and released from the supporting structures of the limb in the act of driving and carrying the horse forward.

Overtrack   Or "tracking up," the horse's hind feet step on or ahead of the front prints.

Pace   The variations within the gaits such as working trot, extended trot, collected trot; a goal (in dressage) is that the tempos should remain the same for the various paces within a gait. (Pace also refers to a specific two-beat lateral gait exhibited by some Standardbreds and other horses.)

Power   Propelling, balancing (and sometimes pulling) forces.

Rapidity   Promptness, quickness, the time consumed in taking a single stride.

Regularity   The evenness in cadence, the rhythmical precision with which each stride is taken in turn.

Relaxation   Absence of excess muscular tension.

Rhythm   The cadence (beat) of the footfall within a gait, taking into account timing (number of beats) and accent. This is similar to the time signature of a musical piece.

Sprain   Injury to a ligament when a joint is carried through an abnormal range of motion.

Step   A single beat of a gait. A step may involve one or more limbs. In the walk, there are four individual steps. In the trot, there are two steps each involving two limbs.

Stiffness   Inability (i.e., pain or lack of condition) or unwillingness (i.e., bad attitude) to flex and extend the muscles or joints.

Strain   Injury (usually to muscle and/or tendon) from overuse or improper use of one's strength.

Stride, length of The distance from the point of breaking over to the point of next contact with the ground of the same hoof; a full sequence of steps in a particular gait.

Suppleness Flexibility.

Suspension The horizontal floating that occurs when a limb is extended and the body continues moving forward; also refers to the moment at the canter and gallop when all limbs are flexed or curled up, reorganizing for the next stride.

Tempo The rate of movement, the rate of stride repetition; a faster tempo results in more strides per minute.

Travel The path of the hoof (limb) flight in relation to the midline of the horse and the other limbs; usually viewed from the front or rear.

FACTORS THAT AFFECT MOVEMENT

Besides conformation and training, there are a number of other factors that can significantly affect a horse's movement.

Pain Even if a horse shows conformational traits that theoretically are associated with straight, sound travel, if he experiences a degree of pain in any portion of his body, he may break the conformation rules as he attempts to use his body in a manner that creates the least stress and pain. An injury or soreness in a limb or an associated structure can cause a horse to protect one portion of the limb when landing, subsequently altering the arc of the foot's flight. For example, if a horse is sore in the navicular region of his front feet, instead of landing heel first and rolling forward, he may land toe first, which will shorten his stride.

Supporting Limb Lameness
Head Movement at the Trot

Lame Limb	Head Down When These Limbs Land	Head Up When These Limbs Land
Right front	Left front/right hind	Right front/left hind
Left front	Right front/left hind	Left front/right hind
Right hind	Left front/right hind	Right front/left hind
Left hind	Right front/left hind	Left front/right hind

Although not absolute, the above is true in many cases. Note the potential confusion between right front and right hind supporting lameness and left front and left hind supporting lameness when using head movement at the trot as the sole indicator.

When a horse is off in a part of his body other than his hooves or limbs, his balance during movement may be negatively altered as he compensates for his pain or soreness. Back soreness can mimic a lower limb lameness and alter foot flight. A variety of other factors can cause the horse to carry his body in a stiff or crooked fashion: muscle cramping, a respiratory illness, a bad tooth, an ear infection, poor-fitting tack. Sometimes the stiffness or pain is low level but enough to prevent the horse from tracking straight.

Imbalance   Impure movement often occurs simply because the horse is trying to keep his balance. He is attempting to keep his limbs under his center of mass. Basically, there are three forces at work when a horse moves: the vertical force of the weight of the horse and rider, the horizontal force of the horse moving forward, and the swinging or side-to-side motion of the horse at various gaits. Exactly where under his body a horse places his limbs is determined in a large part by the interaction of these three forces and the direction of their composite. A barefoot horse moving free in a pasture rarely interferes. It is when he carries a rider and is asked to turn, perform in collected and extended frames, and at both faster and slower speeds that interfering occurs.

A rider can make a horse move well or poorly. Rider proficiency will determine how the horse distributes his weight (from front to rear and from side to side); how the horse changes the speed of the stride or the length of a stride within a gait; and how the horse adapts the stride when turning, stopping, and performing such maneuvers as lead changes. Inadequate riding skills exaggerate the deficiencies in a horse's conformation and way of going. Since no horse is perfect, nor moves perfectly at all times, it takes a knowledgeable and competent rider to compensate for a horse's shortcomings. A rider's balance and condition as well as talent, coordination, and skill at choosing and applying the aids greatly affect a horse's coordination. A horse must be warmed up in a progressive manner before asking him for more difficult work.

Often, inexperienced riders will ask a "cold" or poorly conditioned horse to do three things at once, like come to a hard stop from a thundering gallop, make a sharp turn, and lope off in the opposite direction, without properly preparing the horse or helping him perform in a balanced fashion. When a horse is asked to do something he is not physically ready to do, such as a flying lead change, a deep stop, a fast burst out of the roping box, any kind of lateral work, a tight landing after a jump, or a sharp turn, he can easily become imbalanced.

An unskilled rider can easily throw off a horse's balance formula. Inexperienced riders often commit one or more of these imbalance errors: sit off to one side of the saddle, often with a collapsed rib cage and hip; ride with one stirrup longer; ride with a twisted pelvis; lean one shoulder lower than the other; hold one shoulder farther back than the other; or sit with a tilted head. All of these postures can affect the horse's composite center of mass and can cause him to make adjustments in order to stay balanced. Riders that let their horses ramble in long, unbalanced frames, heavy on the forehand, also seem to have more forging problems. Some horses are able to compensate for an imbalanced rider without forging or interfering, others are not.

Some horses just have an imbalanced way of going. Certain horses are uncoordinated, inattentive, and sloppy while others move precisely, gracefully, and balanced. Training, conditioning, and conscientious shoeing can improve a poor mover's tendencies, but some horses, no matter how talented the rider and farrier, will consistently move in an unbalanced fashion.

Shoeing   Recent but improper shoeing can be responsible for poor movement. If a farrier's shoeing style is "long-toe, low-heel," he sets the horse up to move poorly. A more common cause of movement impurities, however, is a horse being overdue for a reset. Eight weeks after shoeing, even if the horse was shod by a world-class farrier, the hooves have likely grown so out of balance that the horse could easily exhibit gait abnormalities. Sometimes just going a week past the horse's needs can adversely alter the gait synchronization.

Footing   The surface the horse is worked on will directly affect his movement. Traction on dirt occurs when the horse's weight descends through the bone columns of the limbs, causing the hooves to drop one-half inch or more into the ground at the same time the soil is cupped upward toward the sole. This happens whether a horse is barefoot or shod. Shoes basically extend the hoof wall, creating a deeper cup to the bottom of the hoof, therefore increasing traction potential in dirt or soft footing.

Ideal arena footing is light and does not stay compressed, so most of it falls out of the hoof readily with every stride. During the work of a very active horse, the dirt literally flies out of the shoes, but a placid horse may not move his limbs energetically enough to release some dirt with each stride. In dry arenas, the moderate amount of dirt in the shoe comes in contact with the dirt of the arena and results in good traction. If conditions are damp to wet, and the footing is heavy, the hooves may pack and mound, thereby decreasing stability and traction. Packed dirt left in for prolonged periods of time creates constant pressure on the sole and can cause sole and frog bruises. Heavy footing (sand, mud, snow, long grass) generally delays front foot breakover. Some performance events have specialized footing requirements, and it is important to note the footing when evaluating a horse's movement.

Traction   How much grip a horse has on the ground will affect how naturally and confidently he moves. In some instances, a horse requires greater traction than would be provided by bare hooves or a standard shoe: an extreme example is tall studs for jumping. Too much traction, however, will cause the hoof to "stick" when it lands, resulting in a shortened, choppy, and jarring stride. In other cases, a horse is shod to *decrease* traction. The reining horse's smooth sliding plate, which can be over one inch wide, allows the horse to "float" over the ground surface during a sliding stop. This decrease in traction can cause a horse to slip during lope work. Optimum traction results in horse and rider safety, increases a horse's feeling of security so that he will stride normally, and can help a horse to maintain his balance in unstable footing such as mud, ice, snow, or rock.

Condition, level of fitness   A horse's overall level of fitness as well as his present energy level will affect the quality of his movement. In general, a horse has fifteen minutes of peak performance whether in a daily work session or at a competition. He is either approaching that peak period or coming away from it. Take this into consideration during your buyer exam and test ride.

A horse predisposed to forge or overreach may likely do so if he is allowed to dawdle around on the forehand during the warmup, if the bridle reins are pulled up suddenly and the horse is put to work when he is cold, if contact is "thrown away" all at once or engagement is allowed to slip away during work, or if the horse is allowed to fall on his forehand immediately following the completion of his peak performance.

If a rider asks too much of a horse in relation to his current physical capabilities or fitness level, many horses will adapt, attempting to comply. If overworked, many horses will continue moving forward but will modify stride to minimize fatigue and discomfort to flexor muscles and tendons. When a tired horse adjusts the timing of the various phases of his stride, it can result in gait defects. If the hindquarters have not been properly conditioned and strengthened, a horse will rely heavily on the forehand for both propulsion and support. This makes it even harder for the already heavily weighted forehand to get out of the way of the incoming hind feet.

Poor condition or fatigue will often cause a horse to fling his limbs aimlessly—he does not have the muscle strength or energy necessary to project his limbs in a controlled fashion. In some cases when a lazy horse moves slowly at a trot, he may move sloppily and carelessly, and this may cause him to occasionally interfere. Requiring such a horse to move out with more energy may smooth out gait defects. This situation can be interpreted as an exception to the general rule that an increase in speed usually brings an increase in the potential to interfere. The amount of weight a horse is carrying can also exaggerate its lateral limb movements. An overweight horse or a heavy rider may cause more side-to-side sway, which will alter the net forward movement.

Age and stage of development   Young horses that do not have fully developed muscles may lack the width of chest, stifle, or hip necessary for straightforward, efficient movement. The movement of yearlings and some two-year-olds may appear uncoordinated. This can be taken into consideration when evaluating a young horse, but not all horses' movement improves with age.

Training One of the main causes of poor movement and intermittent gait defects is inadequate training. One goal of training is to teach a horse to track forward and relatively straight. Until a horse learns to strongly and decisively step up underneath himself, his travel is often wobbly and inconsistent. Working on small circles and lateral maneuvers before a horse is balanced and supple can cause him to make missteps and interfere. Asking a horse to perform advanced movements like the passage, canter pirouette, or turnaround before he is physically developed and trained can increase the possibility of interference and/or injury. These movements are characterized by either higher action, greater speed, or a greater degree of joint flexion, all which tend to increase rotational forces of the limb and the possibility of interference. Gait defects tend to surface with an increase in speed within a gait as well as the extension of a stride within a gait.

Tack A poor-fitting saddle is one of the main causes of back pain and subsequently poor movement. If a tree is too narrow, it will perch on the horse's back and cause pinching and muscular pain. If the tree is too wide, it places the weight of the saddle and rider directly on the vertebrae. If the balance of the saddle causes the rider's weight to be borne by a small area at the withers, the withers may become injured and result in poor forelimb movement. If the saddle is imbalanced to the rear, especially if the saddle is very long, the loin bears most of the weight, and this can lead to back and hind limb problems.

An improperly fitted bit and bridle can cause a horse to carry its head and neck in stiff and unbalanced fashion, which will greatly affect the horse's overall net movement.

Miscellaneous A host of other factors can cause a horse to move in an irregular fashion. Some mares move with stiffness and tension during a portion of their estrous cycle. Horses with dental problems often carry their head and neck in an unnatural position, which affects their overall movement. A sour, balky, or otherwise ill-tempered animal moves with characteristic resistance. Horseflies and nose bots can cause a horse to move with short, tense strides.

Become very involved in analyzing a prospective horse's movement. Begin with an objective assessment of his conformation. Then watch and listen as the horse is led and ridden on a smooth, level surface in a straight line at a walk and trot. View the horse from the front, rear, and side. Use a camera with high-speed shutter to film the horse's movement. Carefully consider all factors that can affect movement. If poor or irregular shoeing is the obvious factor at fault, you could ask the seller to remedy it. Take into consideration any deficiencies in the horse's training or management as you evaluate his movement.

RECOGNIZING DEFECTS

What Is "Ideal" Movement?

When talking about deviations from the normal, the straight foot flight pattern has often been termed "ideal" (see p. 45). The fact is, such a foot flight is ideal only for a horse with ideal body and limb conformation. Horses with imperfections in their structural components, which includes virtually all horses, will each have an "ideal" foot flight pattern that compensates for their individual imperfections. While a particular horse's pattern may not be textbook pretty, it may be the most functional and efficient for that horse. Instead of thinking of the straight foot flight as ideal, think of it as "straight," so that rather than representing a goal, the term indicates a baseline for comparison.

Straight front limb movement starts with a straight bone column and a series of hinge joints all symmetrically conformed and working in a true forward-backward plane. Add to this a balanced hoof, and the result should be a straight foot flight. Since hind limbs nearly always turn out to some degree, hind limbs tend to wing in slightly.

GAIT DEFECTS

Gait defects are abnormalities in movement that consistently occur during regular work. Lateral gait defects (inward or outward swing of a limb) can affect a pair of limbs or a single limb. Conformational components that should be evaluated include (in the front limb, for example) shoulder to rib cage attachment; width of chest; width at knees, fetlock, and hoof; and straightness of forearm, cannon, pastern, and hoof.

The underdevelopment (hypoplasia) of one portion of a joint surface (usually of the knee or fetlock joint) can also cause a limb to exhibit a lateral gait defect. Normally the fetlock and knee joints work in a hingelike fashion, backward and forward in a straight line, parallel with the horse's midline. A hypoplastic joint appears to hinge in a swivel-like motion at an angle to the horse's midline. This arc causes the limb to deviate in flight.

Gait defects involving timing and length of stride are related to how close a horse's front and hind feet come together when the horse is moving. Factors to consider when evaluating these defects include the relationship between height at the wither and height at the hip; the amount of muscling and the width of chest and hips; the length, proportion and shape of topline components; the relationship between the length of the topline to the length of the underline; and the relationship between the length of underline to the length of his limbs. Horses with downhill conformation or short backs and long limbs, and especially those with short front limbs and long hind limbs, are the most likely to have contact between front and hind limbs. Horses with limbs that are close together or toed-out are the most likely to have contact between two front limbs or two hind limbs.

DEFECTS IN TRAVEL

Paddling   The foot is thrown *outward* in flight but the foot often lands inside the normal track. Often associated with wide and/or toed-in conformation. Unsightly but rarely causes interference.

Winging   The foot swings *inward* in flight but often lands *outside* the normal track. Often associated with narrow and/or toed-out conformation. Dangerous because it can result in interfering.

Plaiting   Also called *rope walking*, the horse places one foot directly in front of the other; dangerous due to stumbling and tripping; can be associated with chest-narrow, base-narrow, toed-out conformation or chest-wide, base-narrow, toed-in conformation.

Interfering   Striking a limb with the opposite limb. Associated with toed-out, base narrow conformation. Results in tripping, wounds.

Forging   Hitting the sole or the shoe of the forefoot with the toe of the hind foot on the same side. Associated with low withers and high hip (downhill conformation); sickle hocks with a short back and long limbs; a tired, young, or unconditioned horse; one that needs reset; or one who has long toes and low heels.

Overreaching   Hitting the heel of the forefoot (or other portions of the limb or hoof) with the hind foot on the same side before the forefoot has left the ground. Also called *grabbing*. Often results in wounds and lost shoes. Associated with the same factors listed in forging.

Forging

Forging is a gait defect most commonly detected when a horse is trotting but also occurs at the walk. Forging customarily refers to contact made between a hind toe (hoof or shoe) and a front sole or the toe of a front shoe on the same side. Frequently the contact is made when the hind foot is gliding in for a landing and the front foot is between breakover and the swing phase. If the front foot is delayed in its breakover, the hind foot may arrive before the front foot has a chance to get out of the way. As the front foot begins to hinge, the hoof may swing back and slap the toe of the incoming hind hoof. This creates the characteristic click-click when a shod horse forges at the trot and a dull thwack-thwack if the horse is barefoot. A horse can receive a sole bruise from a single hard blow or repeated low-intensity contact.

Overreaching usually indicates that a front shoe has been "grabbed" or pulled off by a hind or that the hind has injured some part of the front limb such as the heel, bulb, coronary band, or even the fetlock or flexor tendons. A horse that forges or overreaches may be more prone to stumble or fall, especially at the moment when the shoe is stepped on or pulled off. If the conditions that cause a horse to forge are ignored or inadvertently perpetuated, the stride imbalances may progress to overreaching.

Forging and overreaching are indications that the horse's movement is out of balance. Balance can refer to the relationship between the front and rear of the horse's entire body as well as to the relationship between the angle of each hoof and pastern. Balance also involves the relationship between the left and right sides of the horse's body. Most horses have an inherent left-right imbalance, which can cause stiff or crooked movement. Medial-lateral balance refers to the balance between the inside (medial) and outside (lateral) portions of a particular limb. Medial-lateral imbalances of hooves and limbs occur most frequently in the knees, hocks, fetlocks, and hoofs and are implicated as causes of gait defects such as winging in and paddling. Although forging and overreaching are mainly due to front-to-rear imbalances, medial-lateral and left-right imbalances can complicate the problem. Forging is primarily due to imbalance, delayed breakover, laziness, or lack of condition.

Interfering

Interfering is a lateral gait defect, one that involves a regularly occurring, abnormal sideways swing of a limb. Some lateral gait defects result in actual physical contact with an opposite limb. Interfering is frequently associated with narrow and/or toed-out horses. Such chest conformation places the limbs closer together, and the toed-out hoof predisposes the horse to winging or brushing, that is, swinging the limb toward the midline during flight. As one limb swings inward, it passes the opposite limb, which is usually in a weight-bearing position. It is at this moment when contact might occur. The higher up the limb the turned-out deviation is located, the greater the torque imparted to the limb and the worse the winging will likely be.

Interfering can occur at any gait. The speed and energy level with which a horse moves its limbs will have an effect on its tendency to interfere. One horse may interfere at the jog but not at the extended trot; another horse may move with adequate clearance at the jog but not at an energetic trot. Similarly, one horse performing a quiet rein-back might move his limbs carefully, but when asked to speed up the back, his limbs might swing from side to side and collide. Another horse may work his limbs with pistonlike precision while backing quickly and straight but might exhibit a clumsy, uncoordinated foot flight if asked to slow down.

Interference can occur from the knee to the hoof of the front limbs and usually from the fetlock to the hoof of the hind limbs. If a horse does not wear protective boots, the first signs of interference may be pain, heat, or swelling in the area of contact. The problem may escalate to include missing hair, bruises, cuts, lesions, chronic sores, and perhaps underlying bone damage.

Legs and protective boots should be examined after a workout and points of contact noted. However, just because contact was made with a boot or leg wrap does not mean that contact would have been made without the protective gear because the thickness of the boot may be the safe tolerance in which the unbooted horse would work.

Sometimes a horse will show reluctance to perform certain maneuvers that have caused him to hit himself in the past. He may try to avoid circular or lateral work by stiffening the back, and working with short, hopping strides with the hind limbs. With a reining horse, interference problems in the front limbs may make him reluctant to add speed to his turnaround.

Paddling

Wide-chested and/or toed-in conformation is associated with paddling: The foot is thrown outward in flight but often lands inside the normal track; contact is rare. Often balancing the hooves and encouraging breakover to occur where the hoof "wants" to break over will diminish paddling. If paddling continues once the hooves are balanced, yet the horse is sound and does not interfere, paddling should be considered normal movement for that horse.

(Refer to *Maximum Hoof Power* in the appendix for more information on gait defects.)

Chapter Five

Evaluating Temperament, Behavior, and Training

You can learn valuable information about a horse by carefully observing him in his stall, pen, or pasture as well as when he is being handled, groomed, and tacked up. Keep an eye out for signs of any bad habits or vices. Look for clues to health problems.

> **Vice**   Abnormal behavior in the stable environment that results from confinement, improper management, or weak character. A vice can affect a horse's usefulness, dependability, and health. Examples are cribbing, weaving, and self-mutilation.
>
> **Bad habit**   Undesirable behavior that occurs during and is usually a result of (poor) training or handling. Examples are rearing, halter pulling, striking, and kicking.

SIGNS OF VICES AND BAD HABITS

Wood chewing   Look at stall edges, feeders, gates, rails, noting fresh splinters or areas of damage. Metal gates in a chewer's stall may have the paint stripped from them.

Cribbing   Is the horse wearing a cribbing strap? Look for notches on the tops of posts, on stall doors, feeders.

Stall kicking   In the horse's stall, are there broken boards or dented walls at hock level?

77

Wood chewing

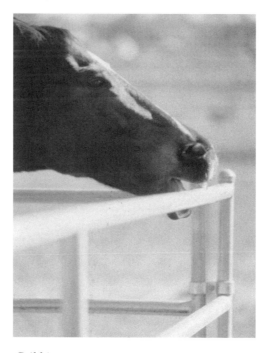

Cribbing

Pawing   Are there holes at the stall doorway or near the horse's feeder? Some chronic pawers are indiscriminate as to where they dig their holes, and it could be in the center of the stall. If the horse is barefoot, the toes of his front feet might be worn abnormally short and dubbed off.

Pacing   Is there a path across the stall doorway, or if the horse is in a pen, is there a deep groove worn along one side?

Pawing

Weaving   Look for pits or worn spots, usually at gateways or doorways.

Tail rubbing   Is the top of the horse's tail ruffled and short?

Dental problems   Is there food on the floor or in the horse's water bucket? Note if the food is partially chewed wads.

Digestive problems   Do the feces show extreme looseness or dryness? Is there blood, worms, or excess mucous in the stool?

Relationship with other horses   Watch as the horse is being led past other horses. Does he put his ears back and dart aggressively toward them or suddenly step sideways to stay out of their reach or scream when separated?

Attitude toward people   If a person approaches the horse when he is in his stall or pen or in crossties, does he look inquisitively with ears forward; does he

Screaming. Life with a herd-bound horse can be less than peaceful.

Vices

Vice	Description	Causes	Treatment
Bedding eating	Eating straw or sawdust	Compulsive eater	Manageable. Must use unpalatable bedding.
Blanket chewing	Chewing or tearing blankets and sheets	Dirty, sweaty coat, shedding, boredom, poor blanket fit	Manageable. Keep horse clean and use properly fitted blanket. If still persists, use muzzle, neck cradle
Bolting	Gulping feed	Greedy or was with competitive horses during feeding	Manageable. Put rocks or large feed wafers in feed tub
Cast	Chronically rolls near stall or pen wall and gets stuck alongside or under panel	Normal causes of rolling: shedding, blanket fit, colic	Manageable. Serious if horse left for long period of time unnoticed, as horse can seriously colic. Bank stall bedding against stall wall; use anti-roller (surcingle-like item) in conjunction with sheet or body blanket.
Cribbing	Anchoring of incisors on edge (post, stall ledge), arching neck, gulping air. Colic, poor keeper (prefers mind drugs over food). Contagious	Theory: Endorphins are released during the behavior; horse is addicted to endorphins, which stimulate pleasure center of brain	Incurable. Cribbing strap prevents contraction of neck muscles; also available with clamps, spikes, electric shock. Possible future pharmacological treatment. Surgery possible. Muzzle can be used in some situations
Kicking other horses	When turned out with other horses, kicks for any or no reason	Hormone imbalance, nasty disposition	May be incurable, as it's difficult to referee. May never be able to turn horse out with other horses
Masturbation	Various methods of self-stimulation and ejaculation in a stallion	Sexual frustration	Manageable. Be sure horse has adequate exercise; can use mechanical devices to prevent erection

Behavior	Description	Cause	Management
Pawing	Digs holes; tips over feeders and waterers; gets leg caught in fence; wears hooves away, loses shoes; most often young horses	Confinement, boredom, excess feed	Curable. Provide exercise, diversion, don't use ground feeders and waterers, use rubber mats, don't reinforce by feeding. Formal restraint lessons
Self-mutilation	Bites flanks, front legs, chest, scrotal area with squealing, pawing, and kicking out. Onset 2 years, primarily stallions	Can be endorphin addiction similar to cribbing; can be triggered by confinement, lack of exercise, or sexual frustration	Manageable/might be curable. Geld nonbreeding stallions; increase exercise, reduce confinement, stall companion or toy, neck cradle, muzzle, possible future pharmacological treatment
Stall kicking	Smashing stall walls and doors with hind hooves, resulting in facilities damage and hoof and leg injuries	Confinement; doesn't like neighbor; gets attention	Can be curable depending on how long-standing the habit. Increase exercise, pad stall walls or hooves, use kicking chains or kicking shoe, don't reinforce by feeding
Tail rubbing	Rhythmically swaying the rear against a fence or stall wall	Initially dirty udder, sheath or tail; shedding HQ, pinworms, ticks, and other external parasites or skin conditions. Later, just habit	Manageable with grooming, cleaning sheath and udder, deworming, other medical treatments. For chronic habit, use electric fence
Weaving/pacing	Swaying back and forth often by stall door or pen gate. Repeatedly walking a path back and forth	Confinement, boredom, excess feed, high-strung or stressed horse	Manageable. Turn out where he can see other horses. Use specially designed stall door for weaver
Wood chewing	Gnawing of wood fences, feeders, stall walls, up to 3 lbs. of wood per day	Lack of coarse roughage in diet, boredom, teething	Manageable. Increase roughage in diet. Decrease palatability of wood. Cover wood with sturdy metal, or use electric fence to deter. Increase exercise and activity. More time out on the pasture.

Bad Habits

Bad Habit	Description	Causes	Treatment
Balking	Refusal to go forward often followed by violent temper if rider insists	Fear, heavy hands, stubbornness, extreme fatigue	Curable. Review forward work with in-hand and longeing. Turn horse's head to untrack left or right. Strong driving aids with no conflicting restraining aids (no pull on bit). Do not try to force horse forward by pulling—you'll lose
Barn sour/herd bound	Balking, rearing, swinging around, screaming and then rushing back to the barn or herd	Separation from buddies or barn (food, comfort)	Curable but stubborn cases require a professional: a confident, capable trainer who insists the horse leave the barn (herd) and then positively rein forces the horse's good behavior so horse develops confidence. The lessons "Go" and "Whoa" must both be reviewed
Biting	Nibbling with lips or grabbing with teeth, especially young horses	Greed (treats), playfulness (curiosity), or resentment (irritated or sore). Investigates things with mouth. Often from hand-feeding treats	Curable. Handle lips, muzzle, and nostrils regularly in a businesslike way; when horse nips, tug on chain, then resume as if nothing happened. Can also use tack on sleeve, hold wire brush toward lips or use muzzle
Bolting when turned loose	Wheels away suddenly before halter is fully removed	Poor handling, anxious to exercise or join other horses	Curable but dangerous, as horse often kicks as he wheels away. Place treats on ground before you remove halter; use rope around the neck

Problem	Signs	Causes	Cure
Bucking	Arching the back, lowering the head, kicking, or leaping	High spirits, gets rid of rider or tack, sensitive or sore back, reaction to legs or spurs	Generally curable; monitor feed and exercise; proper progressive training; check tack fit
Can't catch	Avoids a person with halter and lead	Fear, resentment, disrespect, bad habit	Curable. Take time to properly train, use walk-down method in small area first, progress to larger. Remove other horses from pasture; treats on ground, never punish horse once caught
Can't handle feet	Swaying, leaning, rearing, jerking foot away, kicking, striking	Insufficient or improper training. Horse hasn't learned to cooperate, balance on three legs, take pressure and movement of farrier work	Curable but persistent cases require a professional. Thorough, systematic conditioning and restraint lessons: pick up foot, hold in both flexed and extended positions for several minutes while cleaning, grooming, rubbing leg, coronary band, bulbs, etc.
Crowding	Pushing into the handler in the stall or while being led	Poor training and manners	Curable with proper restraint training (use of chain)
Halter pulling	Rearing or setting back when tied, often until something breaks or horse falls and/or hangs by halter	Rushed, poor halter training, using weak equipment or unsafe facilities—so horse gets free by breaking something. Often horse was tied by bridle reins	Can be curable but very dangerous and incurable in some chronic cases, which require a professional. On advice of a professional, might use stiff-bristled broom in the rump or wither rope
Head shy	Moves head away during grooming, bridling, clipping, vet work	Initially rough handling or insufficient conditioning, painful ears, or mouth problems	Curable. First eliminate medical reasons such as ear, tongue, lip, or dental problems. Start from square one with handling; after horse allows touching, then teach him to put head down

Bad Habits

Bad Habit	Description	Causes	Treatment
Jigging	Short, stilted walk/jog with hollow back and high head	Poor training, attempts at collection; horse not trained to aids, too strong bridle aids, sore back	Curable. Check tack fit, use aids properly, including use of pressure/release (half halt) to bring horse to a walk, or use strong driving aids to push horse into active trot
Kicking	Lashing back at a person with one or both hindlegs, also "cow kicking," which is lashing out to the side	Initially reflex to touching legs, then fear (defense) of rough handling or to get rid of a threat or unwanted nuisance	Might be curable, but serious cases are very dangerous and require a professional to use remedial restraint methods. Unlikely to ever completely cure
Rearing	Standing on hindlegs when led or ridden, sometimes falling over backwards	Fear, rough handling; doesn't think he must go forward or is afraid to go forward into contact with bit; associated with balking; a response to collected work	Can be curable, but is a very dangerous habit that might be impossible to cure even by a professional. Check to be sure no mouth or back problems. Review going forward in-hand with a whip and review longeing
Refusal to load	Balking, rearing, or backing up when asked to step into a trailer	Poor training	Curable with progressive lessons in leading, restraint, "Whoa," and "Walk on"

Behavior	Description	Cause	Remedy/Notes
Running away/ bolting	Galloping out of control	Fear, panic (flight response), lack of training to the aids, overfeeding, under-exercise, pain from poor-fitting tack	Might be curable but very dangerous as when horse panics, can run into traffic, over cliff, through fence, etc.; remedy is to pull (with pressure and release) the horse into a large circle, gradually decreasing the size
Shying	Spooking at real or imagined sights, sounds, smells, or occurrences	Fear (of object or of trainer's reaction to horse's behavior), poor vision, head being forcibly held so horse can't see, playful habit	Generally curable. Put horse on aids and guide and control his movement with driving and restraining aids
Striking	Taking a swipe at a person with a front leg	Reaction to clipping, first use of chain or twitch, restraint of head, dental work	Curable but very dangerous, especially if coupled with rearing, as a person's head could be struck
Stumbling	Losing balance or catching the toe on the ground and missing a beat or falling	Weakness, lack of coordination, lack of condition, young, lazy, long toe/low heel, delayed break-over of hooves, horse ridden on forehand, poor footing	Curable. Have hoof balance assessed, check breakover, ride horse with more weight on the hindquarters (collect), conditioning horse properly
Tail wringing	Switching and/or rotating tail in an irritated or angry fashion	Sore back from poor-fitting tack, poorly balanced rider, injury, rushed training	May not be curable once established. Proper saddle fit, rider lessons, massage and other medical therapy, proper warmup and achievable training demands

turn and move away; does he turn his hindquarters toward the person or put his ears back in a "You're not welcome" gesture?

EVALUATING GROUND TRAINING

Entering stall or pen   Does the horse turn his head or hindquarters to you when you enter his stall? Does he walk up to you or head to the farthest corner?

Catching   Is he easy to catch and halter in the stall, pen, or pasture, or do you have to corner him or use tricks?

Leading   Does the horse stay in position next to your shoulder? Does the horse lag behind or pull ahead? Does he swerve, spook, or stop? Does he need a chain? At both a walk and trot in-hand, is he under control?

Tying   Can the horse be safely tied to a post or put in crossties without swerving, pawing, whinnying, pulling, or chewing? Will he stand quietly tied for a half-hour or more?

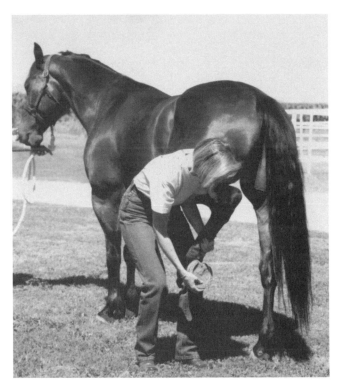

Although this horse lifts his foot cooperatively for the buyer, he nibbles the seller's arm. Although the buyer didn't notice this, her agent did, which is a good reason to bring along another observer on your buyer exams.

To assess balance, rhythm and flexibility, ask the seller to longe the horse at a canter in a 60-foot-diameter circle. . .

a 40-foot-diameter circle. . .

and a 20-foot-diameter circle.

Working on feet   Does the horse cooperate for his hooves to be picked up, picked out, and for the farrier to shoe him? Does the horse lean, rear, jerk his feet away, fall down, nibble, or hop around?

Loading in the trailer   Does the horse walk straight into a trailer? Can he travel in a regular single-horse stall, or does he require a double stall or extra-large trailer?

Longeing, or ground driving   Watch the horse for five minutes in each direction as he is longed at a trot on a 60-foot-diameter circle. Then have the circle decreased to 15 feet and evaluate his attitude and trot movement (does he speed up and become unbalanced, or does he collect?). Watch him canter a 60-foot-diameter circle and then have the circle decreased to 40 feet for two circles, then 20 feet for two circles. Did the horse continue cantering? Was he balanced, rhythmic, well behaved? Was his breathing normal?

Clipping   Can the horse be clipped (bridle path, under jaw, legs, etc.) without a twitch, or does he resent having his head handled?

Grooming   Does the horse enjoy being groomed, or is he irritated by it? Does he have any untouchable areas? Can you use a vacuum on him?

Bathing   Does the horse allow hosing and bathing procedures without being restrained?

Veterinary work   Is it easy to deworm the horse? Does he put up a fuss for vaccinations? Does he cooperate with the vet for dental work?

Handle the horse's head to see if there are any untouchable areas.

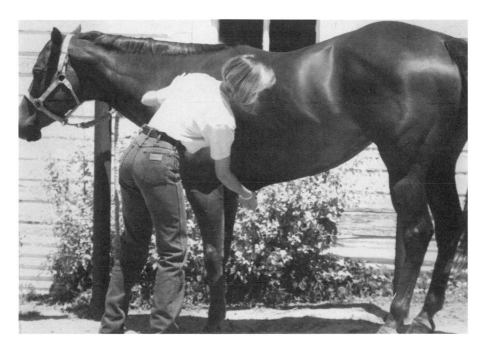

Does the horse enjoy grooming?

Saddling   Does he stand still for saddling and accept the tightening of the cinch without being grouchy?

Bridling   Is he cooperative about having his head handled, or is he head shy? Does he willingly take the bit, or is he stiff jawed? Does he try to rub on you when you bridle him, or does he move away when you present the bridle to his face?

EVALUATING A HORSE'S RIDING TRAINING

Let the owner or regular rider demonstrate the horse's riding ability first. If you have brought your instructor or trainer along and he or she wants to ride the horse before you do, use the time for observation. While the horse is being ridden, watch for the following signs of the horse's temperament under saddle and the thoroughness of his training:

Is the horse tense or relaxed? Tension is often evident by grinding of teeth, swishing of the tail or holding the tail very rigidly, bobbing the head, rushed gaits. The signs of relaxation are a contented expression, a swinging back, a tail that swishes back and forth with the movement of the hindquarters, a soft working of the bit in the mouth with salivation, and either regular or periodic blowing or snorting.

Does he hold his head steady, or does it bob? Nodding can indicate lameness. See "Supporting Limb Lameness" (table), chapter 4, p. 67.

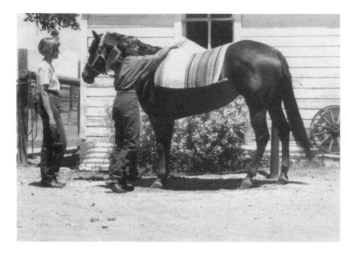

What is the horse's reaction to a blanket?

Does the horse stand still for saddling?

What is the horse's reaction to the tightening of the cinch?

Does the horse stand still for the application of fly spray?

Ask if you can bridle the horse.

Is his back flat, arched slightly up, or hollowed? Generally, a hollow back indicates the horse has a sore or weak back and is dipping it away from the rider's weight. A horse that slightly bows his back up to meet the rider's seat is comfortable carrying a rider's weight.

Does the horse move forward? When the rider asks, does the horse readily step forward or move from one gait to the other with cooperation, or is he balky or resistant?

Let the owner demonstrate any special skills the horse may have, such as this horse, which was taught to sit for mounting!

Note the horse's manner for mounting.

Is the horse's rhythm regular? You evaluated the horse's movement earlier in hand. Does he maintain an even tempo when ridden, or does he speed up and slow down or have an irregular cadence to one or more of his gaits?

Does the horse accept appropriate contact with the bit? Does the horse willingly reach his neck and mouth forward to take a soft contact with the bit, or does he raise his head (get above the bit), or bring his head toward his chest (get behind the bit), or drop his head very low to avoid contact with the bit? Contact, accomplished properly, occurs when the rider's driving aids cause the hindlegs to step up under the horse's supple back and the resulting energy meets the soft but steady restraining influence of the rider's hands on the horse's mouth.

Is the bit that is used on the horse a legal bit for show purposes? Is any other kind of illegal tack being used during the demonstration ride?

Does the horse move relatively straight? If you stand along the arena rail and watch the horse move directly toward or away from you, is his body straight, or are his hips offset to his forehand, causing his legs to travel on three or four lines of travel. (This of course does not apply to horse's being ridden in lateral movements where the goal *is* multiple tracks.)

Is the horse balanced from front to rear, or does he travel heavy on his forehand? His conformation or style of training may set him up for this.

Does the horse pick up the correct lead at the canter, or lope in both directions? When he canters, does he show good reach (viewed from side) and straight body alignment (viewed from front or rear) on both leads?

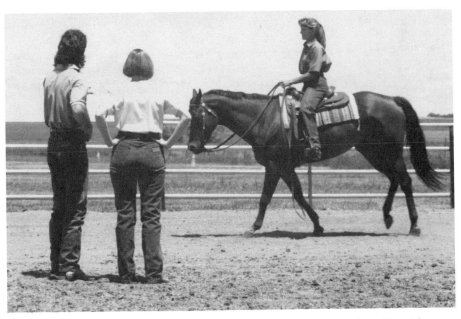

With your agent, evaluate the horse's training and movement as the seller rides.

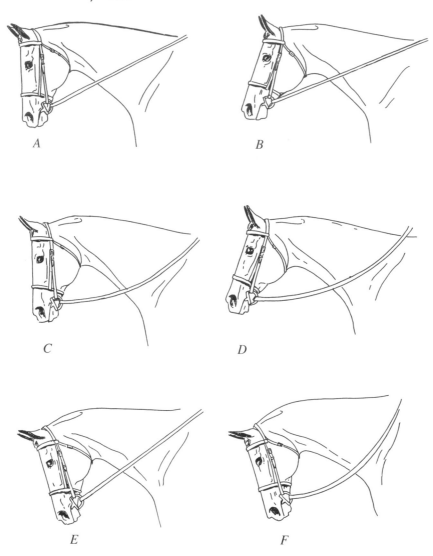

Is the horse on the bit? From Hill, Making Not Breaking.

A = *moderate to strong contact on the vertical and is probably on the bit (OK for intermediate English horse)*

B = *moderate to strong contact in front of the vertical and could be on the bit or above the bit (OK for beginning English horse)*

C = *light contact at the vertical and is probably on the bit (OK for intermediate Western horse)*

D = *light contact in front of the vertical and could be on the bit or above the bit (OK for beginning Western horse)*

E = *strong contact behind the vertical and probably behind the bit (not desirable)*

F = *no contact behind the vertical and behind the bit (not desirable)*

The energy and configuration of this horse's head and neck show characteristics of a dressage horse that is on the bit.

As he gets into the work session, is his breathing steady, rhythmic, and quiet or are there gulps, gurgles, or rattles?

Is the horse prompt is his responses?

Does he show any balking, bucking, nervousness, or shying?

Ask one of the riders to work the horse on sloping or irregular ground so you can assess his coordination.

THE TEST RIDE

Be sure to wear riding clothes and a protective helmet on the day you are to take the test ride. Ask if it is all right for you to use your own saddle, providing it fits the horse. This will give you a better means of evaluating the horse, since you won't be experiencing a different horse and different saddle at the same time.

Notice whether the horse stands perfectly still for mounting. Does he dip his back when you settle in the saddle?

When he walks off, does he look forward alertly with a happy expression to his ears, or does he hold his head in a grumpy or lazy manner?

Before you take a test ride, ask the seller any last-minute questions. (Although this rider is not wearing a protective helmet, it is advisable to do so.)

Note the horse's manners as you mount.

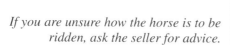

If you are unsure how the horse is to be ridden, ask the seller for advice.

Trot for ten to fifteen minutes. Is he willing to move immediately into a balanced trot, or does he lurch into it, requiring you to pull him back? Or do you need to repeatedly ask for the upward transition before you get a response? Does he have an even, cadenced stride? Watch his head movement. Is he comfortable to sit or post? Is he easy to turn at the trot?

Change rein at the trot on large figures: across the diagonal, in a large figure eight, on a serpentine, and determine if he feels even on both reins in both directions.

Ride a 10- to 15-foot circle at the sitting trot or jog to see if he stays balanced or if his shoulder falls in or he throws his hindquarters out.

Get a feel of the horse's mouth at the jog.

Does the horse lope on the correct lead, and is the lope comfortable?

Ask for a turn on the hindquarters.

Does the horse back willingly?

Canter five to ten minutes. Were his departs prompt and on the correct lead? Is he easy to turn at the canter? What is the speed of his canter? Too fast, too slow, or just right? Is he comfortable so that you feel you are sitting level or slightly uphill, or does he have an uncomfortable downhill way of carrying himself? Is his breathing regular? Canter several large circles (60 feet) and then one or two small circles (20 to 40 feet) to see how balanced he feels.

Ask if another horse can come into the ring along with the one you are testing. How does he behave with another horse in the ring?

Ask if you can test him for the specialized work you have in mind, such as jumping, trail obstacles, advanced dressage movements, or reining maneuvers.

Ask if you can ride him out of the arena first without another rider and then with another horse along. How independent and confident does the horse appear when out of the arena?

Ride up and down a slope if possible to see how he uses his hindquarters. If a slope is not available, trot him actively forward, then bring him to a prompt halt, noting how he uses his hindlegs. Does he place them well under his belly in a fluid motion, or does he stab them into the ground with a jerk or leave them loose and strung out behind his body?

Ask if you can ride the horse out of the arena. How independent and confident is the horse when he is away from his stablemates?

SUMMARY OF BUYER EXAM

Buyers usually don't ask questions about a horse they are looking at for fear of sounding ignorant, of offending the seller, or of hearing an answer they don't want to hear. Don't ever feel that you are stupid for asking a question or repeating a question if you don't get a clear answer. Unscrupulous sellers might try to intimidate a buyer by an impertinent reaction to a question. If so, then there might be more than the answer to that particular question that you should avoid.

Most sellers don't object to any questions posed respectfully unless they have something to hide about the horse. If you are worried about offending a seller, just explain that the more information you gather on the horse, the more smoothly the pre-purchase exam will go. If you have found a horse that is perfectly suited to your needs and the next step is a pre-purchase exam, you may want to fill out a horse information sheet like the one below and have the seller look over the information you have recorded to be sure it is accurate. The veterinarian might ask the seller to sign the sheet or a similar one the vet fills out at the time of the exam.

If you do not ask questions about a horse because you are afraid you will hear something that will make you not buy the horse, it is way past the time for you to have an objective expert give you an opinion on the horse. Sometimes, due to frustration or impatience or because you have "fallen in love" with a horse, you might purposely be overlooking a major health condition or behavior abnormality.

To be sure you haven't forgotten anything, go over the following checklist to see that all is in order. As you ask the questions, be wary of absolute statements such as "This horse would never kick," because anyone who has been around horses knows that any horse can kick and that it seems that horses do understand English and love to prove blanket statements incorrect.

HORSE INFORMATION CHECKLIST

Horse's name _____ Breed _____

Date of birth _____ Sex _____

Color and markings _____

Brands or other permanent ID _____

Registration number _____

1. How long have you owned the horse?
2. Where did you get him?
3. What have you used him for and what is his level of training and performance?
4. Does the horse have any vices?
5. Does the horse have any bad habits?

6. Has the horse had any injuries?

7. Has he ever been lame?

8. Has the horse had any surgeries?

9. Has the horse had any illnesses or other health problems such as laminitis, colic, or allergies?

10. Has the horse ever been on medication?

11. Is he now?

12. When was he last vaccinated, with what, and by whom?

13. When was he last dewormed, with what, and by whom?

14. When was he last shod and by whom?

15. What is the horse being fed?

16. Has the horse been nerved?

17. Has the horse had any tail alternations?

18. Has the horse been tested for EIA, HYPP, or other diseases? If so, what are the results?

19. Why is the horse for sale?

20. How long has he been for sale?

Signed _____ (owner or owner's agent)

Date _____

Chapter Six

The Pre-Purchase Contract and Veterinary Exam

If you have found the perfect horse, you'd like the seller to hold the horse for you. When a horse is put on hold, he is essentially taken off the market. That's why it is to the seller's and buyer's mutual benefit to draw up a pre-purchase agreement. Such a contract will indicate your serious intent and outline terms of the sales agreement. It might also state a limit to the number of times you may try the horse and a deadline for your decision. A pre-purchase contract clarifies a buyer's rights and obligations.

THE PRE-PURCHASE CONTRACT

Usually a deposit is required in addition to your signature. A deposit can reduce risks for both parties. A deposit can compensate the seller if you do not buy the horse and he loses a sale to another customer because the horse was off the market while you were further considering him. Alternatively, the buyer may insist on an arrangement that requires the seller to refund the deposit if the buyer elects not to buy the horse within a specific time. A deposit provides both parties a guarantee that the horse will not be sold to anyone else while the contingencies of the contract are being met. The contract also fixes the price at the one originally quoted. A well-designed contract is really a protection for both the buyer and the seller.

In most states, the Uniform Commercial Code (UCC) requires a written sales contract for any goods costing over $500. A Pre-Purchase Agreement (or

If you want an exclusive hold on a horse, most sellers require a pre-purchase contract.

Contract to Purchase or Sales Contract) can satisfy this requirement. Confer with your agent about the laws of buying and selling horses in your state.

NOTES ABOUT ITEMS COVERED IN A CONTRACT TO PURCHASE OR PRE-PURCHASE AGREEMENT OR SALES CONTRACT

PARTIES   This agreement is made between _____,
(name and address) hereinafter referred to as BUYER and _____,
(name and address), hereinafter referred to as SELLER.

[*Note: seller's name should be listed exactly as it is on the horse's registration papers to avoid transfer problems.*]

STATEMENT OF THE PURPOSE OF THE AGREEMENT   This agreement is entered into between BUYER and SELLER for purchase and sale of the horse described below on the following terms and conditions of sale:

DESCRIPTION OF HORSE   Registered Name_____

Registration Number and Association _____

_____

Tattoo, brand, or other identification (state which) _____

_____

Date of Birth _____Sex_____

Color and Markings _____

hereafter called the HORSE.

PRICE.   For the total sum of $_____, SELLER agrees to sell BUYER the HORSE described here and BUYER agrees to buy said HORSE on the terms set forth here.

PAYMENT TERMS.   A deposit of $_____(10% of purchase price) is to be paid at time of offer. This deposit will hold the HORSE for the BUYER for _____days or until the results of a veterinary pre-purchase exam are available whichever is sooner. This deposit is not refundable if the HORSE is described as serviceable for BUYER'S purpose and BUYER does not complete the purchase. This deposit is refundable if the veterinarian fails to find the HORSE serviceable for BUYER'S intended use. BUYER'S intended use is

_____.

The balance of the purchase price $_____ shall be paid by the BUYER at time of possession, no later than _____days from the date of veterinary results. The form of payment must be cash only (*or list other acceptable alternatives*). Daily board from the time of offer to the time of possession at the rate of $_____per day is also due at time of possession.

[*Note: There may be a statement about retail sales tax since 45 states impose a tax on some horse transactions. Check with your agent. Usually, if tax is necessary, buyer pays and seller must collect.*]

CONTINGENCIES.   This contract is contingent on the described HORSE passing a veterinary pre-purchase suitability examination by Dr. _____ at the BUYER'S cost with the intended use for the HORSE being stated as _____. BUYER understands that the offer is based on the fact that BUYER has knowledge that the HORSE has the following blemishes, unsoundness, conformation defects, vices, or unusual behaviors

_____

_____

_____

BUYER states that he knows what the above conditions represent and although discussion of them with a veterinarian is encouraged, since the conditions have been previously noted and accepted as exceptions by the BUYER, the conditions stated above can not be basis for canceling this contract and receiving a refund of the deposit.

If the HORSE is found to be not serviceable, the BUYER's deposit will be refunded in full.

WARRANTIES.   SELLER warrants that he has clear title to the HORSE and will provide a bill of sale, appropriate registration transfer papers, and necessary health and transport papers at time of possession (*or payment, stipulate which*). Risk of loss passes from SELLER to BUYER at time of possession (or payment, stipulate which). The terms of this agreement are governed by the laws of the state of _____. This contract is the final and entire agreement between the parties.

THE SELLER MAKES NO EXPRESS WARRANTIES AND DENIES ANY AND ALL IMPLIED WARRANTIES OF MERCHANTABILITY OR FITNESS FOR A PARTICULAR PURPOSE. THE SAID HORSE IS SOLD "AS IS."

The SELLER makes the following warranties regarding HORSE:

_____

Signed this _____day of _____, 19_____

_____   _____

   (Seller)   (Buyer)

[*Important notes: Every state has its own laws regarding the necessary content of contracts. Generally such a contract can not be made with a minor but must be made with the minor's parent or legal guardian. This group of contract notes are designed to provide you with general guidelines. Check with your agent or attorney or modify a standard sale contract purchased from a business or stationery store to fit your specific needs. A knowledgeable attorney should be consulted regarding the particular requirements of contracts in your state.*

Negotiable items include: price, what vet is used, who pays for vet, deposit percentage, method of payment, length of contract, when risk of loss passes.

Additional items include: who provides transportation, agent's commission, who pays attorneys fees in case of a suit, arrangements for a trial period, where a suit (if brought) must be filed, or whether disputes, if any, must be submitted to binding arbitration, etc.]

THE VETERINARY EXAM

A pre-purchase veterinary examination is often a contingency in a written sales contract or an informal contingency in a verbal offer. The prospective buyer selects the veterinarian, schedules the exam, and pays for it. In order to avoid conflict of interest, and to encourage a truly impartial exam, the veterinarian should not be the seller's regular vet. The information obtained during a pre-purchase exam should be summarized in writing. It may be necessary for the buyer to formally request this from the veterinarian. The written report becomes the property of the person who paid for it, the potential buyer. If someone else, such as the seller, wants a copy, the only way he should be able to get it is through permission from the potential buyer. It is privileged information contracted between the veterinarian and the prospective buyer. Often both the owner and the seller are present during the pre-purchase exam. With the permission of the buyer, the veterinarian can verbally report findings throughout the examination.

If you are at all concerned about a horse's health or soundness, he should have a thorough pre-purchase exam performed, especially if you are inexperienced. It is not wise to accept a seller's claim that the horse has already been "vetted" because all that might mean is that at some time the horse was looked at by a veterinarian.

A pre-purchase exam is a fact-finding session and can be a useful tool for both the buyer and the seller. It is not a guarantee, an insurance policy, or a value appraisal, and it is not a certificate of ability, temperament, or merit. It is a physical examination for evaluating health and serviceability on a particular day. It is a window in time. A pre-purchase exam should not be thought of as a soundness exam (a term used in the past) because the term tends to give a false sense of insurance for the future. All horses have defects. Any horse can develop a future unsoundness or health problem.

The pre-purchase exam should be performed at the horse's home barn by an equine veterinarian with the buyer present. It is best for the seller to be present also to answer questions on the health history of the horse. The better the equine practitioner, the more valuable the results of the exam. Beware of using a veterinarian that is a specialist unless that specialty is specifically why you hired him or her. For example, some equine veterinarians specialize in reproduction and might not have as broad a base of experience in equine lameness as another vet.

You also may wish to retain the opinion and services of a qualified farrier. The greatest emphasis in the examination of a riding horse is centered around the legs and hooves. In examining the hooves, the veterinarian may request that the shoes be removed, so it may be necessary to schedule a farrier to be present to pull the shoes and to reshoe the horse. Also, the farrier can often shed additional light on such hoof-related problems as severe cracks, sole bruising, underrun heels, club feet, evidence of founder, etc. In this case it might be best to talk with the horse's

As you test ride the horse, you may detect an uneven-ness or imbalance in his movement.

You might want to confer with a qualified farrier to see if there might be a hoof-related problem.

regular shoer but have a qualified, unbiased farrier look at the horse as well. (See *Maximum Hoof Power* in the appendix for more information.)

The results of the exam are more reliable when conducted on a horse that is physically fit and in regular work. If a horse has been idle, he may appear sound during the exam, but if purchased and put into serious work by the new owner, he may develop problems.

Pass or fail?   The American Association of Equine Practitioners (AAEP) guidelines for reporting purchase exams suggest that "the veterinarian should list all abnormal or undesirable findings discovered during the examination and give his or her qualified opinion as to the functional effect of these findings."

If a veterinarian is very concerned about not offending the seller and passes a horse with a cursory clinical examination, there could be problems for everyone. This can pose a real threat for the veterinarian because the courts often take the position that if a veterinarian calls a horse "sound" or "suitable for intended purpose," he or she may be liable if an autopsy reveals that the horse had a pathological process.

The AAEP suggests that "the veterinarian should make no determination and express no opinion as to the suitability of the animal for the purpose intended. This issue is a business judgment that is solely the responsibility of the buyer that he or she should make on the basis of a variety of factors, only one of which is the report provided by the veterinarian."

Veterinarians approach pre-purchase exams in various ways. Since most liability claims against veterinarians are not based on *incorrect interpretations* of findings but on *failing to disclose* findings, some vets go over a functionally sound horse with a fine-tooth comb, pointing out every blemish and irregularity and read the X-rays with an air of impending doom. They are trying to protect themselves. While this approach may keep a vet safe from legal action from either party, it often kills the sale. Such an approach is not only hard on the seller but also on the buyer, who may be scared away by a long list of what might actually be acceptable irregularities that have technically intimidating names.

Therefore, the ideal situation for all parties is communication and cooperation. Ahead of time, develop with the veterinarian a reasonable level of "perfection" that the horse must exhibit for the use you have in mind. Ask the vet to describe potential problems and together decide on which tests should be administered. The veterinarian then performs the tests and reports the results. You, the buyer, then decide whether the horse passes or fails the pre-purchase exam based on your previous criteria and the results of the tests. This is the best type of pre-purchase exam, but it does take preparation and time.

If a horse shows a significant problem after a sale, some buyers complain to a veterinarian, "Why didn't you tell me about this?" That's why it is best to set up your custom needs ahead of time, communicate throughout, and make sure the reports are in writing.

Excepted conditions   Before the exam, such as when you are conducting your buyer exam or test ride, a seller might point out a condition of the horse that could cause it to "fail" a veterinary serviceability exam but would still allow it to be suitable for a particular buyer's purpose. One example of this would be a cribber. A horse might be a good riding horse but have the incurable habit of cribbing. If it is something you can accept and are willing to manage, then cribbing might be listed on the pre-purchase agreement as an exception to the forthcoming exam.

Another example is an infertile mare. She might be a suitable mount but would fail a breeding evaluation. If you and the seller have discussed such a condition and you agree that it is not important to your use of the horse, the seller might want you to agree that it is an exception to the findings of the pre-purchase vet exam. That means if everything checks out all right on the horse, except for the previously excepted condition(s), you have essentially accepted the horse "as is." It is important to understand this distinction because your veterinarian might strongly suggest you do not buy the horse because of the condition. But if you have already signed an agreement accepting the excepted condition, the seller might be entitled to keep your earnest money deposit because you acknowledged and accepted the condition. That's why it is important that you fully understand any habit or condition the horse has before agreeing to accept it.

BE ON THE LOOKOUT FOR THESE CONDITIONS

Lameness-related problems such as

Arthritis   Early stages can be managed; end-stage joint inflammation and degeneration cause loss of use.

Bowed tendons   Thick, bulging flexor tendons; depending on severity, may or may not be serviceably sound; prone to reinjury.

Navicular syndrome   Forelimb lameness from mild to severe; often treatable with proper shoeing.

Laminitis (founder)   Horses that have had a severe bout with laminitis make poor performance choices but can make acceptable breeding animals. Mildly affected horses, if managed correctly, might return to some level of use but may be at increased risk to refounder.

Cracks   Deep, vertical cracks extending to the coronary band can be a red alert, especially if there is a moist discharge from them. It can be time-consuming and costly to restore such hooves. Superficial cracks are usually of no concern.

Spavin   Enlargement of the hock; can be fluid or bony growth. Depending on the stage of the spavin, the horse could be sound or lame.

Nerving   A severing of the nerves to give the horse relief from pain in that foot. May be evident as small scars at the back of the pastern. May be unsafe as a riding horse. With careful management can be a breeding animal.

General Health problems such as

Heaves   Labored breathing caused by dust and allergies that results in poor performance (easily winded). The heave line (a thickened muscle line on both sides of the horse's abdomen) is caused by the abdominal muscles pushing air out of inelastic lungs.

Melanomas A slow-growing cancerous tumor of the pigment-producing cells. Generally not curable. Common on the head and under the tail in older gray horses.

Moon blindness A chronic, recurrent inflammatory eye disease that often leads to blindness.

Parrot mouth Incisors that exhibit an overbite causing eating difficulties and dental problems.

Hernia umbilical or scrotal hernias are fairly common in foals, but many heal (retract) without treatment by two months of age. Those that don't will require veterinary treatment, usually surgery.

BLEMISHES

Blemishes usually do not affect serviceability, but ask your vet to examine each one.

Proud flesh Tumorlike mass over wound site on lower limbs that can inhibit movement; can be treatable depending on location and severity.

Sarcoid Scaly or wartlike virus invasion of tissue, often around head; often reoccurs following treatment.

Splints Lumps on the inside or outside of cannon bone; usually a self-correcting condition; if horse is not lame, no problem.

White spots Patches of white hair at site of old injury or areas of pressure, such as at withers; if inactive, no problem.

Capped hock or elbow Fluid-filled area over the point of the joint that might have been caused by lying down on hard ground or from stall kicking.

Old rope burn A crusty ridge, often at the rear of the pastern; may cause stiffness and crack open occasionally; usually curable.

Warts Rough bumps on the muzzle that eventually disappear with or without treatment; common in young horses.

Windpuffs Fluid fillings of the fetlock joint or tendon sheath; may be normal and sound operating state for that horse. Occasionally can indicate a problem.

TESTS AND EXAMINATIONS

There is no standard pre-purchase examination. Inform your veterinarian of your intended use for the horse and any special concerns you have. Then together, with economics relative to the horse's price in mind, you can decide what tests will be necessary to make such a determination. The exam will take from an hour to several hours or more. Costs for an exam can run from $100 to $1,000, depending on the number of radiographs required, what lab tests are ordered, how many miles the veterinarian must travel, and how much time is involved in the exam. The findings of the exam should be made in writing.

General clinical exam   An overall health check is the minimum that should be performed. First the veterinarian must identify the horse using markings, brands, and registration papers. Then he should get a thorough history of the horse from

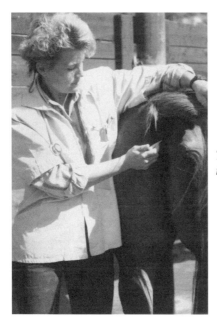

The general clinical exam includes taking the temperature.

The pinch test for dehydration

the owner including such information as vaccinations, deworming, previous illness or injury, surgeries, previous X-rays taken, breeding records, and any vices or unique problems. If you recorded this information during your buyer exam, you can provide the information to your veterinarian to save time and money. The seller may be asked to sign the report.

Some veterinarians make an examination of the horse's pen or stall for clues to general eating habits, fecal consistency, and telltale signs of such vices as cribbing, wood chewing, pacing, pawing, stall kicking, and weaving.

The veterinarian next performs what is often called a general physical or clinical examination: The vet looks at, listens to, and touches (palpates) the horse. After palpation and observation, the veterinarian can provide a report or continue with more specialized tests as requested. The following are often included in the general physical:

- Temperature, pulse, and respiration before and after moderate exercise. The resting heart rate can be a general indicator of temperament: A high rate might indicate a nervous horse or it could indicate an ill or unconditioned horse.

- Gastrointestinal exam with a stethoscope to determine if there is normal gut function.

- Heart exam both before and after exercise with a stethoscope to detect murmurs or irregular rhythm. Arrhythmia could indicate heart disease, infection, or hereditary defect. Such a horse could have decreased stamina.

A heart exam

- Lung exam with a stethoscope to evaluate lung sounds. Some veterinarians might ask the seller to place a plastic bag or a special rebreathing bag over the horse's nose to cause the resting horse to breathe more deeply and make irregularities easier to detect. (It is important that the horse is familiar with a plastic bag near his head before this exam or his respiration rate will not be the only thing that will rise suddenly!)

- Dental exam checking the teeth for bite alignment, missing teeth, the presence of wolf teeth, and any sharp edges on the molars that may need to be floated. It can usually be determined if the horse is a cribber by the condition of his incisors. If the horse's age is in question, the veterinarian can determine the age by the teeth. While near the upper respiratory area, the vet also checks for abnormal odors (tooth abscess), sounds, or discharges and looks at the tongue for signs of lacerations.

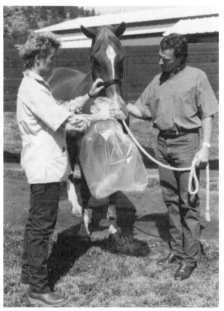

A lung exam, which may include the use of a rebreathing bag

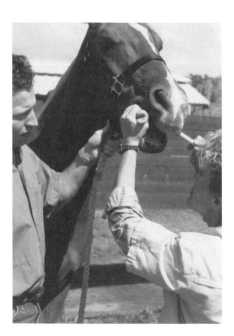

Dental exam

Capillary refill time

- Capillary refill time (general circulatory indicator): The finger is pressed on the horse's gum and it is noted how long (number of seconds) before blood returns to the circular spot.
- Eye exam includes checking for inflammation and scars on the retina, cloudiness of the cornea (the clear covering at the front of the eye), cataracts on the lenses (loss of transparency in or on the lens), or other abnormalities. Also, the pupils' response to light is tested. This is best performed in a dark

An eye exam.

stall: Normal pupils will dilate in darkness and will constrict in the presence of light. Usually an eye doctor's flashlight (transilluminator) is used.

A magnifying device is then attached to the transilluminator, making it an opthalmoscope for checking the interior of the eyeball. The vet looks for various problems including uveitis (moon blindness), which is a chronic disease that has an active and non-active phase and that often leads to blindness. If a horse has a history of excessive tearing or blinking in bright light, it is possible he may suffer from moon blindness. This condition may occur in one or both eyes. It varies in severity and the length of time before blindness occurs.

- Skin exam for scars, fungus, or other skin conditions.
- Back palpated for any soreness or swelling. The horse's spine should be evaluated from head to tail. A normal horse dips his back from palpation in the saddle area and pushes upward on palpation of his croup.
- Lymph nodes palpated to check for swelling that indicates problems.
- Tail checked for any surgical alterations.

Examination of the Limbs

Lameness is one of the most important portions of the exam, especially for a performance horse. For a thorough discussion of limb examination and lameness diagnosis, see *Horseowner's Guide to Lameness* in the appendix. Some lameness can be managed with regular, preventive shoeing and medication, while other lameness is hopeless.

For the limb exam, the veterinarian will probably want to watch the horse being longed on a hard, flat surface.

- *Conformation evaluation*   Although a veterinarian rarely gives an opinion on the potential of a horse as a halter prospect, he or she does want to look at the horse from all angles to assess symmetry, balance, and to spot any potential problems.

- *Movement*   Usually before specific limb tests, the veterinarian watches the horse move in-hand in a straight line, on the longe line in a circle, and possibly under saddle. Gait defects show up more markedly in the circle required by longeing and under a rider's weight than they do when the horse is merely being led. Often a vet requests that the horse be worked on both a hard, flat surface as well as in deep, soft footing.

- *Palpation*   The lower limb structures (bones, flexor tendons, suspensory ligaments) are palpated before and after exercise for any heat, swelling, hard lumps (bony growths), tenderness, or a pounding pulse. The veterinarian usually spends a fair amount of time palpating the superficial and deep flexor tendons and suspensory ligament to determine if there is any current problem or evidence of an old problem. They should be of an even thickness, without heat, bulges, or adhesions.

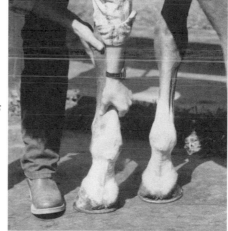

Palpation of the lower limbs

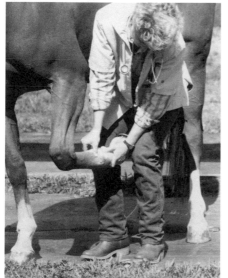

Looking for tendon problems

The use of hoof testers is often a part of the exam

A flexion test to the front limb

Hock flexion test

- *Hoof exam* Each hoof should be visually examined in a static position from the front, side, and rear to assess balance. Each hoof should be picked up, and using what is necessary (hoof pick, hoof knife, hoof testers), all of the structures of the hoof should be evaluated: the frog, clefts, sole, wall, heels, white line, bulbs of heel. Any sensitivity, foul odor, cracks, rings, heat, abnormal shape, or other irregularities should be noted. The quality of shoeing should be also noted, as well as the presence of what might be therapeutic farriery, such as full pads, wedge pads, etc. (See *Maximum Hoof Power* in the appendix.)

- *Hoof tester* Most exams include the use of a hoof tester, which administers pressure to assess sensitivity in different portions of the hoof, including the navicular area. A hoof tester must be used by an experienced veterinarian. Misapplication can give false results.

- *Flexion tests* Flexion tests are performed most commonly to the knees pasterns, fetlocks, and the hock-stifle-hip. First the vet watches the horse move without prior joint manipulation to establish a baseline. Then the veterinarian or an assistant holds the joint in a flexed position for one or two minutes and asks the handler to trot the horse off immediately on a loose lead so as not to constrain head movement. Lameness, stiffness, or irregularities in rhythm or stride are noted and may indicate the need for further evaluation. Some horses that have nothing wrong with their joints will trot off stiffly for one or two steps. Flexion tests uncover painful arthritis (degenerative joint disease) and other problems.

    As the veterinarian picks up each limb to perform the flexion tests, he or she will also be checking each joint's range of motion and sensitivity to reasonable sideways movement, rotation, and pressures. Flexion tests might be performed twice: once when the horse is cold and later when the horse is warm (after exercise). Response is often improved on a thoroughly warm horse.

- *Ultrasound* Occasionally ultrasound imaging is used to evaluate the condition of the flexor tendons and other soft tissue structures.

- *X-rays* If palpation, hoof testers, or flexion tests raise suspicion, the veterinarian may suggest X-rays. Since the cost for X-raying each area runs between $60 and $80, X-rays are limited to joints that suggest degenerative bone problems or arthritis. Most commonly X-rayed are the front feet, all pasterns and fetlocks, and the hock. The horse's shoes must be removed for X-rays involving the foot.

    Not every unsoundness shows up on an X-ray, and not every abnormal mark on an X-ray indicates an unsoundness. An abnormality on an X-ray of a horse that shows no sign of lameness may mean nothing significant. Previous X-rays of the same area may help to spot a progressive problem.

If the clinical exam raises suspicions, the veterinarian might recommend X-rays.

The radiographs of many horses over the age of twelve show some signs of arthritis even though the horse may be perfectly usable.

This is particularly important in considering the possibility of navicular syndrome. The X-rays of a sound horse might show evidence of "navicular changes," yet the horse might stay sound the rest of his life. For example, the X-rays of the navicular bones of sound, three- and four-year-old warmbloods might show "lollipops," which could be alarming to some people. Yet practitioners experienced in warmblood characteristics often feel these are part of the normal bone development sequence in slow-maturing breeds.

On the other hand, a horse that is very lame and shows many of the classic signs of navicular syndrome might have normal-looking X-rays. It is also important to note that two veterinarians might "read" an X-ray in two very different manners. Therefore, in certain situations it may be wise to seek a second veterinary opinion or have the X-rays viewed by a veterinary radiology specialist.

- *Nerve blocks*   Nerve blocks are not routinely performed during a pre-purchase exam on performance horses unless requested by the buyer and permission is granted by the seller. Nerve blocks are more of a lameness diagnostic tool. If a horse shows lameness, it is assumed that the pre-purchase exam is "off" and a lameness exam, now at the seller's expense, is "on."

- *Neurological exam*   To detect the presence of certain neurological problems, the vet may perform some simple tests on horses at risk. Wobbler syndrome is common in Thoroughbreds, and atlanto-occipital instability occurs most frequently in Arabians. To determine if a horse suffers from one of these conditions causing a lack of coordination, he might ask that the horse be led in tiny circles or that the horse be stepped up and down from a trailer or an elevated doorway or be led over ground rails. Horses that have neurological problems might step on their own feet or stumble and be unsafe to ride.

Laboratory tests:

- *Coggins*   One of the most common blood tests is the Coggins test, which checks for the presence of equine infectious anemia (EIA) antibodies. EIA (also called *swamp fever*) is highly contagious. A positive test indicates that the horse has been exposed to EIA in the past and is a potential risk. This test costs about $20, and the results take about three days. Since a current negative Coggins test is usually required for transport in and out of most states as well as for entry in various competitions, most sellers have one on file for any horse that is for sale.

- *Blood chemistry panel*   A variety of disease conditions can be revealed. For example, kidney and liver function can be checked.

- *CBC*   Sometimes a complete blood count is recommended if a horse is anemic or suspected of having an infection. This test includes hematocrit and hemoglobin concentration and measures the oxygen-carrying capacity of the blood. It also reveals if the horse has an elevated white blood cell count, which could indicate infection.

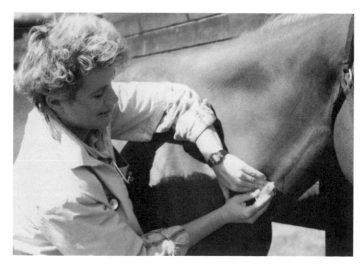

The veterinarian might take a blood sample for laboratory tests.

- *Chemical test*   If you suspect that the horse is under the influence of an unreported drug to make him appear sound or calm, a blood chemical evaluation can be performed for about $75. This can detect the presence of a nonsteroidal anti-inflammatory such as phenylbutazone or Banamine, as well as various behavior-altering tranquilizers.

- *HYPP*   Hyperkalemic periodic paralysis is an incurable but often manageable genetic disorder of horses with Impressive (Quarter Horse) bloodlines. For more information on testing for and management of HYPP, contact your veterinarian and see the resource guide in the appendix.

Other tests that are not routinely done but may be requested:

- *Endoscopic exam*   A respiratory exam with a fiberoptic endoscope can be performed. An endoscope is a flexible tube that is passed through the horse's nostril and functions like a periscope to allow the vet to inspect the upper airway. The exam may reveal scarring or polyps in the pharynx and larynx that could interfere with the horse's breathing. Paralysis of the larynx leads to the condition called *roaring,* which is a heritable condition common in Thoroughbreds. Roaring results from nerve damage to the recurrent laryngeal nerve, causing one side of the larynx to be paralyzed. A relatively straightforward surgery can correct the condition. An endoscopic exam would be recommended for a horse that will participate in strenuous sports such as racing, endurance, eventing, polo, or steeple chasing. Any horse that makes any unusual noise in the upper airway during exercise should be examined with an endoscope.

- *Electrocardiography*   For further, more specific examination of the heart. It measures electrical conducting activity of the heart, which controls the heartbeat.

- *Echocardiography*   An ultrasound examination that allows visualization of the heart while it is beating (thickness, valve closure, blood flow, defects) as well as allowing measurement of heart size (larger heart, larger cardiac output).

- *Computed radiography*   An extremely high resolution X-ray for detecting subtle problems in both bone and soft tissue.

- *Nuclear scintigraphy (bone scan)*   A lameness diagnostic tool that involves the preferential uptake of a measurable radioactive substance in areas of inflammation or injury.

- *Rectal palpation*   Some exams include a rectal exam to detect abnormal growths or sensitivity of reproductive organs and intestinal organs within reach. There is the potential hazard of a rectal tear, so the exam must be approved by the seller. The vet can extract fresh fecal material if a laboratory fecal exam has been ordered. The feces is also checked for consistency, odor, color, and the presence of blood, parasites, or undigested grain.

- *Reproductive exam*   If you are purchasing a horse for future use as a breeding animal, certain examinations should be performed in addition to the above.

Mares often require a rectal palpation, ultrasound imaging of the uterus and a culture and biopsy of the uterus. Some of these tests are invasive and carry risk so must be specifically requested by the buyer and approved by the seller. A rectal examination is designed to detect any abnormalities or sensitivity in the reproductive organs. An ultrasound examination of the female reproductive anatomy gives the vet a means to visually assess tissue condition and the possible presence of fluids in the uterus. A uterine culture is performed to determine if the mare carries an infection. A swab is passed through the cervix and gathers uterine fluids. This sample is examined under the microscope and is also grown on culture medium to identify any harmful organisms and to determine treatment if necessary. A uterine biopsy gauges the relative health of the uterine tissue. A small

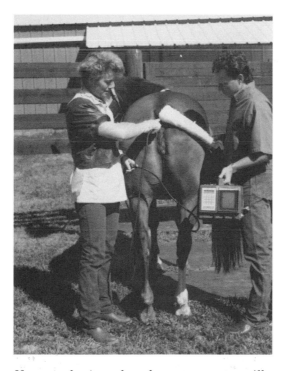

If you are buying a broodmare prospect, you'll want a reproductive exam performed, including an ultrasound of the uterus.

portion of uterine tissue is snipped and examined microscopically in the laboratory. Such a test helps determine whether a mare's uterus is capable of carrying a foal to term.

Stallions should be checked to determine if both testicles are descended because the sperm in testicles that are retained in the body cavity are dead. Stallions being purchased for breeding should go through a full stallion evaluation where semen is collected and examined for content, quality, and viability.

Approximate Charges

Veterinary Exam

Description of service	Cost in dollars
Call charge to farm (depends on distance)	30.00
Pre-purchase exam minimum charge	84.00
Blood sampling charge (for tests below)	15.00
Coggins test (EIA serology)	15.00
Blood chemistry panel (equine diagnostic panel)	20.00
Complete blood count	15.00
Drug test for bute, ace, etc.	75.00
HYPP test	35.00
Electrocardiography	20.00
Echocardiography	75.00
Nuclear scintigraphy (bone, one primary area)	160.00
Ultrasound examination, variable. Minimum	10.00
Rectal palpation	13.00
Mare reproductive exam with biopsy and culture	75.00
Stallion evaluation	200.00
Fecal exam	12.00
X-ray coffin joint	60.00
X-ray navicular region	70.00
X-ray hock	65.00
X-ray knee	72.00
X-ray cannon bone	60.00
X-ray pastern joint	60.00
X-ray fetlock joint	65.00
Computed radiography, in addition to X-ray charge	25.00

Guaranteed?   Remember, a pre-purchase exam is not an insurance policy. Even if a horse is considered serviceable after undergoing a thorough pre-purchase exam, there is no guarantee that the exam uncovered all potential problems or that the horse will remain sound. This is especially true of a horse that has been out of work for some time. After the results are in, be sure to discuss them with the veterinarian. Now is the time to ask questions, not two months after you have the horse at your barn.

When a horse has cleared the vet check, you will have a certain number of days (three, for example) to complete payment and pick up the horse. During this time it is the seller's responsibility to have the horse cleared by a brand inspector in states where it is required. The seller must also have the necessary transfer papers available so that at the time of sale, the registration papers can be signed over to the new owner.

If the horse passes the veterinary serviceability exam and you do not follow through with the purchase, the deposit is normally forfeited to the seller for the inconvenience and the time the horse was off the market. If the horse does not pass the veterinary serviceability examination, your deposit is refunded or the horse's price can be negotiated in light of the veterinarian's findings.

Trial period   If everything looks good after the exam, some sellers consent to a trial period of a week to a month. However, sending a horse to live away from home while he is still technically not sold is very risky for the seller. That is why the seller will probably insist to have in writing the exact terms of the trial period agreement, such as who provides the insurance, what veterinarian and farrier will work on the horse, and who foots the costs during the trial period.

Chapter Seven

Paperwork and Legalities for the Buyer

Insurance is a good idea if you can't stand the risk of losing your investment in the event of the death or serious injury of your horse. Your horse's insurance should be binding when the risk of loss passes from the seller to you. If you bought your horse at an auction, the terms will state when the risk of loss occurs, at the fall of the hammer or at time of possession. When a horse is purchased through private treaty, the contract of sale should specify whether risk of loss passes when the money has been paid by the buyer, when the money has cleared the seller's account, when the horse is in the buyer's possession, or when the title has been transferred. These are especially important distinctions when you buy a horse but leave it in training with the trainer who sold the horse. It is also important in the case of the purchase of a suckling foal when the foal stays with the dam.

INSURANCE

Sellers who offer an installment contract (down payment with monthly payments on the balance) usually require that the horse be insured during the term of the sales contract. The cost of the policy is usually paid for by the buyer.

The amount of the policy is usually the purchase price of the horse including sales tax and, in some cases, the cost of transporting the horse from the point of purchase. An offer to purchase, unless accepted, is not sufficient to prove an

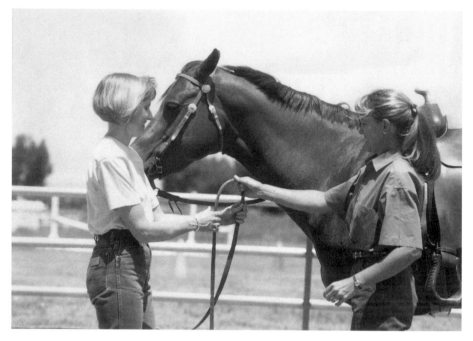

Before the seller can turn over the reins to you, there is some paperwork that must be completed.

increase in value. If the horse is homebred rather than purchased, the value of the horse is often twice the stud fee. The policy amount can be increased after the sale by proof of increase in value due to one or more of the following factors:

- Training fees (the company might add half the cost of the training fees onto the horse's price)
- Show or race winnings
- Winnings by offspring
- Sale of offspring
- An appraisal or quality exam by an acceptable appraiser (breed association judge or appraiser acceptable to the insurance company)
- Geographic location

Sentiment or replacement cost are not a part of the value.

TYPES OF INSURANCE

Mortality insurance pays the value of the policy (unless there is a dispute as to the true value of a horse) if the horse dies or if the insurance company agrees that the sick or injured horse should be put down (humanely destroyed). Limited or restricted policies cover specific situations only, such as death by fire or lightning. Full mortality insurance covers all causes of death, including illness and injury. A thorough physical examination is required before a full mortality policy is issued, and even if the horse passes the examination, the insurance company may have standard exclusions for certain causes of death, such as colic.

Various "riders" (addenda) can be added to mortality policies. A permanent loss of use rider pays a predetermined amount if the horse becomes permanently unable to be used for a previously stated use. In some cases, the insurance company may have the option to take possession of the horse.

Other riders include surgical, major medical, and unborn or prospective foal coverage (see chart on page 130). In addition, if you own a horse you should be sure you are covered by a personal or professional liability policy. Many homeowner's policies would cover you if your horse got out on the road and damaged a vehicle or injured a person. If you have a commercial operation, you should check to be sure you have adequate liability coverage. Do not assume that your homeowner's policy will cover losses arising out of your business pursuits. In fact, most homeowner's policies specifically *exclude* coverage for business pursuits.

Insurance rates are based on the value of the horse and vary according to the breed, age, and use of the animal. An accurate statement of use is important because some insurance companies will not cover death occurring while the horse is in use for polo, hunting, jumping, racing, or gaming.

In general, annual policy premiums (rates) range from 1 percent to 6 percent of the policy value of the animal. So, if you are insuring a $10,000 horse and the rate is 3 percent, you will pay $300 for the policy each year. Some riders cost a flat fee.

Application for insurance requires a signed owner application and a completed and signed veterinary exam form. The owner application asks such questions as:

- What type of fencing do you have?
- How often do you deworm and what type of dewormer do you use?
- Has there been infection or contagious disease on the premises in the last 12 months?
- How many of your horses have died or been destroyed in the last 3 years?
- Are there any encumbrances on this horse?
- Is there any indebtedness due because of the change of ownership on this horse?
- Have you ever been canceled or refused insurance?
- Is this horse insured now? Has he ever been insured? With whom?
- Who will be providing care for this horse?

Equine Insurance General Information

Type	Coverage	Requirements	Comments	Premiums
Full mortality	Death by sickness or accident; may cover proven theft (90–100%); humane destruction clause allows vet to destroy horse without approval by insurance company; postmortem may be required; death by poisoning may or may not be covered	Veterinary certificate less than thirty days old. Owner application. May be available for all ages or specified range such as 2–14	Minimum policy usually $100–150; binding when check and satisfactory application received; might have a guaranteed renewal clause for one year or longer	Based on age, breed, and use. Usually 3–7% of the value of the horse. Be sure to read exclusions to coverage and requirements to keep policy in effect.
Limited mortality	Usually death by accident only, such as transportation or other specifically named peril, e.g., fire, lightning, theft, earthquake, floods, building collapse	Same or less than above	No sickness coverage; not commonly a good buy	Approximately 1% of the value of the horse or more
Loss of use	Covers when various causes of sickness or accident render horse permanently unable to perform but horse does not die	Must carry full mortality and surgical or major medical; must state specific use; may require specific tests and X-rays	Policy pays a predetermined amount, such as 50 to 65% of the horse's value; some policies allow owner to decide whether to euthanize horse or keep horse; exact loss paid depends on this decision	Usually 2–3% of the value of the horse
Unborn or prospective foal	Loss of fetus or young foal to thirty days of age	Must have negative twin exam at twenty-forty-five days with ultrasound; manual pregnancy exam		17% of the value required
Surgical-only	Pays vet's surgery bill for nonelective and noncosmetic surgery; also some (e.g., 25–30%) associated costs such	Must carry full mortality	Maximum claim often is $5,000; might have guaranteed renewal; does not	$85–100 per horse and with a deductible of about $50

	as anesthesia, medication, bandages, hospitalization	cover castration, caslicks, or postmortem	
Major medical	Pays surgical and nonsurgical costs such as lab and diagnostic tests, medical treatment, surgery and post surgical treatment	Must carry full mortality	Usual benefits $3,000–5,000, with some policies having guaranteed renewal; no pre-existing conditions	$120–150 per horse with deductible of $200–300 per occurrence
Personal liability	Covers if horse gets loose and is hit by car; damage to car or passengers; covers if horse damages vet's equipment, etc.		Most homeowner's policies cover; if not, a homeowner, can get horse owner policy or if professional, can get commercial policy	Homeowner's policy very variable according to coverage desired; Horse owner's policy for renters e.g. $200/year for 3 horses.
Commerical liability	Lessons, boarding, etc.		May be cost-prohibitive for small operations	Very variable; $600 per year and up
Care, custody, and control	Injury or death of animal in your care	Must own farm where horses not owned by you are boarded, must operate with approved standard of care	Limits up to $200,000 per animal and $500,000 loss per policy year	Depends on size of operation
Professional errors and omissions	Trainer, instructor, farrier, judge, etc., covered if commit error in providing professional services		Overall coverage up to $1,000,000 worldwide; up to $100,000 per horse	$600 and up per year according to the number of students and/or horses.

Note: This information, based on research with many equine insurance agents, is intended to provide a general idea of how equine insurance works. Check with your agent for details of specific options and plans.

The veterinary exam for insurance will vary depending if the policy will contain riders for surgical or major medical. Some of the things the veterinarian will check include:

- Temperature, pulse, and respiration
- Eyes
- Evidence of bleeder
- Evidence of nerving
- Evidence of laminitis
- Any evidence of blistering, firing
- Past lameness
- Past surgeries
- Fecal exam results
- Castration
- Scars
- Male: castrated or both testicles evident
- Female: mare in foal; past breeding or foaling problems; reproductive exam
- Any vices or bad habits
- Deworming program, parasite problems, colic problems
- Does horse have any congenital abnormality or deformity?
- Results of Coggins test
- Any other medical facts that should be brought to the attention of the company

What Type of Insurance Do You Need?

If you are taking a horse on trial, be sure the horse is covered by a full mortality policy and a major medical policy as well. If the seller already has a policy on the horse, be sure the insurance company is notified that the horse is changing locations for the duration of your trial period. Policies are generally not transferable. If you need to purchase a new policy, be sure it is binding *before* you move the horse from the seller's premises. Some insurance companies issue short-term policies, but most usually issue a policy for an entire year. If you decide not to keep the horse after the trial, you can cancel the policy and get a refund for most of the base policy but probably not the riders. Also, be sure your personal (homeowner's) or commercial liability policy is in force before the horse arrives at your place.

If you are buying the horse on contract, the seller will probably require you to have a full mortality policy on the horse at your expense. Usually both the buyer and seller's names are listed on the policy as loss payees. In the event the horse dies, a check is made out to both of you, and it is up to you to decide how to split it up. It would also be a good idea for you to purchase a major medical policy on the horse.

Deal with an experienced equine agent that is licensed in your state.

WARRANTIES

Warranties outline the responsibilities of the seller and the rights of the buyer. In the past, the selling of horses was ruled by the saying *Caveat emptor*: "Let the buyer beware." The seller was not obligated to inform the buyer about any defects or lack of quality in his animals. That placed the burden on the buyer to keep an eye out for his own protection. Today, the seller must make good his or her representations of facts regarding the horse, where they are used to induce the buyer to make the purchase. In this respect, many believe the selling of horses today is ruled by *Caveat vendor* (or *mercator*): "Let the seller beware."

If a seller makes an express or implied warranty about a horse at the time of sale, it is considered a guarantee. An *express warranty* is a verbal or written statement of fact or promise made by the seller that becomes part of the basis for the sales transaction. Examples are "This is an Olympic-caliber dressage horse," or "This horse never took a lame step in his life," or "This horse can be ridden by anyone." To become an express warranty, the seller, in making these statements, must know of your plans and the horse's abilities. Where this occurs, the seller promises the horse will conform to the description.

The law in most states provides that general statements of "sales talk" or "puffing" about a horse do not amount to express warranties. Examples of puffing are "He's a nice horse," "He'd make a dandy horse for you," or "This mare is well-bred." These constitute opinions, whereas express warranties are promises.

An *implied warranty* is not necessarily stated verbally or in writing but is assumed to be part of the agreement. Common implied warranties include that the seller has the legal right to sell the horse and that the horse is suitable for a particular purpose.

According to the Uniform Commercial Code, all verbal or written statements of the seller become part of the basis of the sale—in effect, a warranty. The burden then is on the seller to carefully and conspicuously exclude statements and promises to the potential buyer if he or she does not intend to be bound by them as warranties.

But this does not mean that you as a buyer do not have to look carefully at the horse you are hoping to buy. If there are defects that can be easily noted by inspection, you are responsible for detecting them. It is up to you or your advisor to note such defects. You cannot later claim one of these obvious defects as a reason to rescind the sale.

If there is a latent defect or one that is not easily discoverable by ordinary inspection, whether or not it can be the basis for rescinding a sale depends on whether the seller knew of its presence.

The horse's suitability for a particular purpose is considered an implied warranty. If you make known to the seller, in clear terms, the purpose for the horse, the seller's selection and presentation of a horse to you amounts to a warranty that the horse is suitable for the disclosed purpose. This is mainly in cases where you are relying on the seller's skill and judgment to furnish a suitable horse. However, be aware that suitable does not necessarily mean successful.

A seller can call various factors about a horse to your attention and exclude those items from a warranty. Those items, then, would not be the basis for rescinding a sale. A seller can also sell a horse "as is" if it is conspicuously stated and understood between parties that the horse is being sold without a warranty.

If you feel you have purchased a horse that has been misrepresented, the best thing to do is first discuss the situation with a knowledgeable and experienced attorney. Then, if advised, approach the seller and discuss the matter with him. Any reputable seller will try to work out a problem regarding a horse sale.

If you must resort to court action to resolve the matter, the burden of proof is on you, the buyer, that is, the law requires you to prove each and every element of your case. If it is found that there was a breach of warranty, you will probably be awarded the difference between the value of the horse as warranted and its actual value. So if you paid $10,000 for a horse that was only worth $6,000, you would recover $4,000. (See chapter 9 for a discussion of the role of the appraiser.) You may also be able to recover costs for other losses, expenses, or damages, such as feed, medicine, veterinary bills, and others. In some cases, your attorney might be able to rescind the sale.

The interpretation of the law often hinges on the determination of who is a "merchant." A "merchant" means a person who deals in horses or otherwise has the knowledge or skill peculiar to the horse business and horse transactions. If the seller is a "merchant," then an implied warranty is that the horse is "merchantable." The courts look at cases differently if both the seller and the buyer are knowledgeable horse people, as they would both be classified as merchants under the UCC.

Some transactions involve statements such as "AS IS" and "NO WARRANTY" (in sale catalogs or on sales contracts) that deny any express or implied warranties. The reason for this is that warranties can, in most states, be legally excluded by properly drafted written agreements.

For example, one sale catalog states:

> *All responsibilities and guarantees lie between the buyer and seller. The seller is the responsible party for all representations or warranties, express or implied concerning the condition of any horse and buyers should satisfy themselves concerning the*

condition of any horse they purchase. Except as otherwise announced by the auctioneer at the time of sale, the consignor of each animal represents and warrants to the buyer the following: (1) Title of the animal free from all adverse claims to ownership, use or possession. (2) The animal is sound of eyes and wind.(3) The animal is not a cribber or windsucker. (4) The animal has not been nerved, does not have navicular disease, or has not foundered. (5) The sex or condition as a gelding or ridgling is as described in the sale catalog or announced at time of sale. (6) Any animal which at time of sale is described as a colt and does not at such time have two testes descended to the scrotum must be announced. Warranty with respect to descended testes does not apply to any horse sold prior to July 1 of his yearling year. If any of these conditions is announced, the consignor is held harmless for the condition. Except for the foregoing limited warranties, each animal is sold by the consignor WITHOUT WARRANTY AND WITH ALL FAULTS. Every horse is sold under this rule, therefore, no horse can be rejected by the buyer when struck off by the auctioneer.

If you are buying a horse, beware of "AS IS" or "NO WARRANTIES" clauses as the seller is not guaranteeing anything. For example, if you are buying a horse for a specific purpose, such as for breeding, the sale documentation should clearly state, "The seller warrants the mare being sold is fit for breeding purposes and guarantees that the mare is physically able to conceive."

The use of proper language in a sales contract or bill of sale is very important. Depending on the selling price, you might wish to seek legal advice in drafting the terms and conditions of a sales contract according to the laws of the state in which the sale takes place.

OTHER PAPERWORK

When the final sales transaction is being made, be sure that all the necessary paperwork is taken care of before you give the seller your check. If you are not experienced in paperwork matters, bring someone who is along with you (see chapter 12 for more information on paperwork). Registration papers should bear clear title from the seller to you, the new buyer. If the seller is a business (such as a partnership or a corporation), the person who signs the papers over to you should prove that he or she has sufficient authority, and the law might place the burden on you, the buyer, to ascertain this. Be sure the description of the horse on the papers matches the horse you are buying exactly. Brand clearance and ID certification papers should be unmistakably for the horse you are buying. If there is a

In most states, the brand inspector is mobile and makes his inspection at the point of sale.

shadow of a doubt, clear it up before the final sale. Some sellers have been known to use certificates from deceased horses to sell other, less valuable horses.

Beware of registered horses offered for sale by someone who claims to be exercising a "stablemen's lien" or "agister's lien." In many cases, these people have not properly complied with their state's law, and you might find yourself owning a horse with no registration papers.

Horse ownership is proven using state brand board paperwork, brands, tattoos, microchips, registration papers, and bills of sale. Most states have brand boards that are designed to protect livestock owners by providing inspection of animals before and during transport. A "brand" inspection does not necessarily mean that the horse has been hot branded. Even horses that have no identification markings must be inspected. Usually, any time a horse changes ownership, crosses a state line, or is transported over seventy-five miles within the state, a brand inspector must physically inspect the horse and the paperwork and issue a brand clearance. In states without an inspection law, during a sale transaction you must get a bill of sale and health certificate from the seller before you transport the horse. The bill of sale must have the seller's name and signature, the buyer's name and signature, a description of the horse (color, sex, breed, markings, registration number, brands, etc.). The parties may want to have the bill of sale, at the time it is signed, witnessed by a neutral third party to the transaction. Should disputes later arise involving the sale, or even the bill of sale, that witness may be needed to prove that the seller did, in fact, transfer the horse and sign the document.

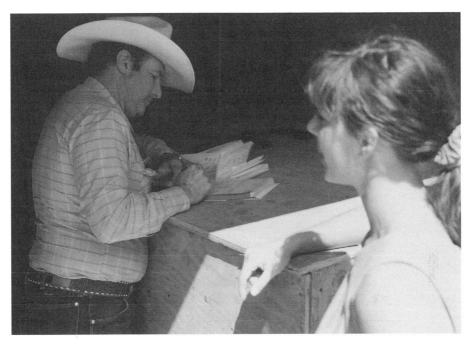

In order for the brand inspector to issue clearance, the seller will need to provide proof of ownership.

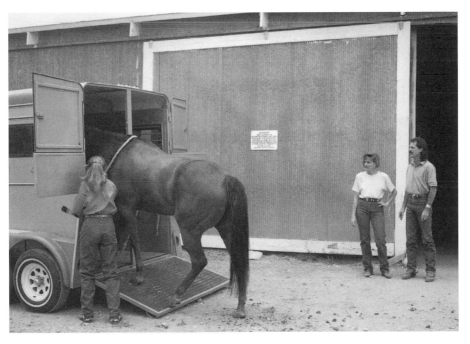

Before you transport the horse, be sure you have the necessary paperwork completed.

Chapter Eight

Alternatives to Buying

INTERNATIONAL BUYING

International buying is an "alternative" because it is basically an exciting, expensive way to spend a vacation! It is only financially wise to consider international purchase if you are shopping for untrained two-year-olds in the $20,000 and over category or four-year-olds and older started under saddle in the $35,000 and over range.

Unless you are a very experienced horseman and very familiar with the country you are visiting and its language, you should hire a contact agent to line up sources in other countries. This agent will eventually collect a 10 percent (approximate) finder's fee on any horse you purchase through his leads. Who pays the agent's commission will be a part of the sale bargaining. In addition to the agent's leads, you can find valuable information by studying horse magazines from the country that deal specifically with the breed or sport you are interested in.

It is most cost effective to do preliminary sorting via phone, fax, photo, or video for several months before you travel to physically inspect the horses. Be sure to take a very savvy horseman along with you, even if you are quite experienced yourself. It is easy to miss important details when trying to communicate in a foreign country.

Expenses for one person to travel to Europe from the United States for a two-week shopping trip, including car rental, lodging, and meals would range from

$3,000 to $5,000 and more depending on the country visited and whether your lodging is rural (lower) or urban (higher).

Your buyer exam should follow a similar format to that described earlier, but local customs of presenting horses might require you to specifically request certain in-hand, longeing, or riding exams. The pre-purchase exam could cost anywhere from $400 to $800, so you will need to know specifically what to request. If you are shopping for a very expensive horse, it might pay for you to take your regular veterinarian along with you.

If you find a horse you want to purchase, you will probably pay by international bank transfer. Arrangements should be made well ahead of your departure from your home country. Any horse purchased should be immediately covered by insurance, and you should be certain the insurance will cover the horse completely during all phases of travel.

Transportation from the seller to the point of export is sometimes locally arranged, but often you can hire the services of an international forwarder (horse transportation agent) to arrange for the horse's transport from the seller to the import point of quarantine. From Europe to the United States, for example, transportation will cost somewhere between $3,500 and $6,000, which includes air fare and all quarantine costs. Sometimes the international forwarder can also provide insurance for the entire trip, plus thirty days after arrival, for about 1 percent of the horse's value (value = purchase price plus commission, freight, quarantine, and forwarder's fees).

When you import a horse from another country, you'll have to pay for pre-importation tests required by law. These tests will reveal such diseases as African horse sickness, dourine, glanders, equine infectious anemia, Venezuelan equine encephalomyelitis, and piroplasmosis. A certificate must be issued on each horse stating the horse is found free of contagious equine metritis (CEM). Geldings and horses less than two years old often will not require an additional import permit if the CEM permit is valid.

Mares and stallions usually must be quarantined for a period (often three weeks) prior to export. All horses must be quarantined at a registered facility at the point of import. Geldings might only need to be quarantined for three days, but breeding animals may need to be observed and tested for five weeks before being released to you.

Leasing

If you can't or don't want to invest in purchasing a horse, you might be able to find a suitable horse to lease. Most leases are made for a period of a year at a time. You would pay the horse's owner an annual lease fee, usually one-third the value of the horse, due at the time of agreement. If you were looking at a $9,000 horse, you would expect to pay $3,000 to lease the horse for the year. A full lease would

Sometimes leasing a well-trained horse is the answer. Photo: Laurie Krause

allow you to use the horse for purposes you and the owner agreed upon. Usually the lessee, you, would be responsible for all maintenance costs: feed, board, farrier, veterinary maintenance. Most lessors (owners) require the horse to be fully insured (by the lessee) during the period of the lease. In the lease agreement, it should be specifically stated what occurs if the horse becomes seriously ill or injured. Would the lease be automatically canceled? Or would you be responsible for caring for the horse during lay-up?

Some owners (usually of less expensive horses) are very flexible with lease arrangements and might lease the horse to you for a much lower cost, absorb some maintenance costs, and even provide you with some tack to use.

Explore the lease with an option-to-buy possibility.

When leasing, be sure to inspect the horse just as thoroughly as you would if you were purchasing him. If you are leasing a broodmare, be sure to have a thorough reproductive exam performed.

A lease agreement should contain the following:

- Names and addresses of lessor (owner) and lessee (person leasing the horse)
- Full and complete description of the horse
- Purpose of the lease: proposed use of the horse; limitations on use
- Length of the lease

- Does lessee have the right to sublease?
- The cost of the lease and when payment is made
- Insurance arrangements including mortality, major medical, surgical, and liability
- An outline of care of the horse
- When veterinary bills exceed a certain amount, who pays
- If horse is seriously ill or injured, is the lease still in effect?
- Under what circumstances can the lessor cancel the lease?
- Under what circumstances can the lessee cancel the lease?
- Warranty by lessor as to ownership, horse's health, suitability, etc.
- Any other specific arrangements such as

    option to buy

    delivery arrangements

    right of lessor to sell horse during lease and if lessee has the right of first refusal

    if there is a sole rider, driver, or handler stipulated

    if there is a trade of formal training of the horse in exchange for the lease fee

    if the horse can be used as a school horse

    automatic renewal option
- Signatures of both parties with dates and witness

Shares, Syndication

Sometimes, with very expensive horses, a joint ownership syndication is a good business strategy. A high-priced breeding stallion might be out of your price range, but together with several friends who also own broodmares, you might make a joint purchase and share maintenance costs of the stallion. A syndication is a form of group ownership, a business partnership. Some advantages include:

- Partners share risk and expense.
- You can diversify by owning shares in several horses.
- You share income from breeding fees or sale of offspring.
- You are ensured a certain number of breeding rights.
- Group ownership may be a more effective way to manage a stallion.

For more information on syndication, see "Horse Industry Directory" in the appendix for the address of the American Horse Council.

Breeding your own horse is an option, but realize that it took five years and $15,000 (not including training) to bring this suckling to maturity.

Breeding

Instead of buying a particular type of horse, you might want to breed your own. This can only be a cost-effective option if you have your own farm and broodmare or access to a very nice broodmare at a reasonable lease price. This is one option you must plan very carefully ahead of time. If you just jump in, you could find the experience very disappointing and unprofitable. Following is an outline of some of the expenses of "creating" your own four year old.

The same horse, same pasture, five years later.

Steps in creating a riding horse	Range of costs
Own or lease a mare	$2,000 to 10,000
Board at home or away, 18 months	$1,800 to 3,600
Reproductive exam	$100
Stud fee	$500 to 2,500
Veterinary fees, breeding, 1–3 cycles	$200 to 600
Foaling expenses	$50 to 150
Raise suckling foal to 6 months	$675
Raise weanling to 24 months	$2,025 (18 months)
Board for 2–4-year-old	$2,400 to 4,800 (24 months)
Training for 2–4-year-old	$1,200 to 7,200 (6–24 months at $200 to $300 per month)
Total cost	$10,950 to $31,650

Note: The following amounts were used:
$100/month for adult at-home board; $200/month for adult away-from-home board; young horse = $3.75 per day for feed, deworming, vaccination, farrier, vet

Adopt a Wild Horse

Between 5,000 and 10,000 wild horses and burros are offered for adoption each year by the United States Department of the Interior, Bureau of Land Management. Most wild horses are offered untrained, straight off the range for a $125 adoption fee. In some locations, saddle trained previously wild horses are available for approximately $650. If interested, you must make application to USDI BLM. If accepted, you will be informed as to when and where the horses will be available. You must be eighteen years old and be able to provide at least a 400-square-foot enclosure 6 feet high with acceptable fencing (stipulated in procedures). You must personally fetch your horse from the holding-pen area in a four-horse trailer and transport him. Certain feeding and health care practices must be adhered to. The U.S. government retains the title to the horse for one year. At that time you are required to send in a letter from a veterinarian stating the horse has received good care in order to have the title of the horse transferred from the U.S. government to you. For more information, send for the pamphlet "So You'd Like to Adopt a Wild Horse . . . or Burro?" from BLM (see appendix).

Working Student

If you can't afford to buy or pay for horsekeeping costs, you can still have an everyday horse experience. One way is to take regular riding lessons. Another is to become a working student. In exchange for cleaning stalls and tack and grooming horses, you might be given riding lessons or permitted to use a horse for pleasure riding. A working-student arrangement requires hard work and commitment from you. The person who allows you to use his or her horse must be reciprocated for the costs of keeping that horse by the work that you do.

Chapter Nine

Getting Ready to Sell a Horse

If you have ever tried to sell a horse, you know that horse marketing is a very competitive business. Marketing is a business plan, and advertising is just one part of it. Marketing includes:

- knowing what you have
- knowing how to present it
- identifying the market niche
- checking out the competition (prices, products, techniques, successes)
- showing what you have to offer that is different or better: a more thoroughly trained horse, lessons with the sale, lower price, installment contract, first month's board free
- setting goals and reasonable expectations regarding the horse's price, the amount of time it will take you to sell him, and the type of owner (home) the horse will go to

Usually there are a good number of horses for sale for every prospective buyer. There is always a large supply of partially trained, out-of-shape, "backyard" horses for sale. It is much more difficult to sell a horse that has not been worked for some time, is overweight, either very lazy or a little bit wild, and not professionally cared for or well presented. It is easier to sell a horse at the beginning of a riding season (spring or early summer) than at the beginning of the feeding season (fall or winter).

Not many potential buyers will take a seller's word that "he's a wonderful pleasure horse (but he hasn't been ridden for five years)" and buy a horse without being able to test him thoroughly.

If you hope to sell your horse, you must get him in shape, highlight his positive attributes, and direct your sales efforts to the specific market for which he is suitable. Don't hope to sell a horse by saying he is a hunt seat prospect if he has never been in the show ring, let alone never had hunt seat training.

Early in your sales efforts you must decide whether you will market your horse locally or nationally, at private treaty or auction, how you will advertise and where, and what price you will ask for your horse.

Remember, unless you are selling a very specific age, type, color or bloodline, there are many other contenders in the marketplace. What makes a horse sell? Quality, training, presentation, performance, appropriate price, and paperwork in order.

FINDING A NICHE FOR YOUR HORSE

How well you are able to identify the perfect niche for your horse is the first step in getting a buyer to give you a call. Once you have determined where your horse fits, let those people know he's for sale. Advertise in the most appropriate place for your horse's breed, quality, and level of training and accomplishments. It would be a waste of money to advertise twenty-year-old Nell, with her big hay belly and shaggy mane in a monthly color glossy horse magazine. See chapter 10 for more information on advertising.

Identify the Buyer

Is your horse suitable for a first-time horse owner? For a 4–H or Pony Club horse? For a person who is ready to upgrade? For someone interested in doing a little showing? For a person who wants to raise a foal? For someone who wants to be able to ride right into the winner's circle? For a casual trail rider? A competitive trail rider? For a working rancher? A competition roper? Identify your market and you will have a much easier time attracting the right buyer.

Once you have a good idea of the type of buyer that would be looking for a horse like yours, try to list in detail that buyer's characteristics. Would your horse fit that buyer's bill? Is the potential buyer an inexperienced eight-year-old girl who lives in the city and wants a horse that she can take lessons on? Or is the buyer a twenty-four-year-old serious dressage rider looking for an upper-level horse? Or is the buyer a thirty-something female with some experience fifteen years ago who wants a horse she can ride in the parks on weekends? The same

If your horse can be ridden by young children in both English and western events, you will have buyers standing in line. Photo: Laurie Krause

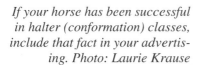
If your horse has been successful in halter (conformation) classes, include that fact in your advertising. Photo: Laurie Krause

horse would probably not be suitable for all of these people, yet quite possibly, your horse might be just the perfect horse for one of them. The more finely you can focus on the type of buyer your horse would be suitable for, the more appropriate your advertising will be.

As you evaluate your horse and describe him, see how he would fare if you had to fill out this "job application" for a riding horse:

- Would you describe your horse as push-button, infallible, unflappable?
- Would he be appropriate for a kid or an absolute novice?
- Can you take him out on a trail ride alone?
- Can he be ridden at the end of a group on a trail ride?
- Will he cross water?

Would your horse be appropriate for a youth's trail horse?
Photo: Laurie Krause

Can your horse be safely ridden out of the arena?

- Is he safe to ride along the highway?
- Has he had any show experience?
    List the classes, number of entrants, and his placings.
- Has he had ranch work experience?
    Give details of the work he has performed.
- What level of training has he had?

    List specifically if competition oriented.
    Will he depart promptly on either lead from both a walk and a trot?
    Does he neck rein?
    Does he perform flying-lead changes?
    How high has he jumped?
    What is his fastest time over jumps, barrels, roping, etc.

- Has he ever lived in a stall? What are his habits?
- Has he been hauled in a trailer? How does he react to loading and traveling?
- Has he ever lived in a pasture alone? With other horses?
- Is he fence wise?

Also, ask yourself why you are selling the horse. Answer honestly so that you don't make any statements to a potential buyer that are not true.

- We don't get along.
- He has a vice.
- He has a bad habit.
- He is intermittently lame at a low level.
- He is frequently "off."
- He is lazy.
- He is too spirited.
- He is too big.
- He is too small.
- He is too expensive to feed.
- He is too expensive to keep shod (requires special shoes).
- He is too expensive to keep in good condition (requires special supplement).
- I no longer want to have a horse.
- I no longer can afford to have a horse.
- Other _____.

International Sales

If your horse is of the caliber and type in demand in foreign countries, you might be able to realize a greater profit by selling the horse abroad (see also chapter 8). Recently, stock horses (Quarter Horses, Paints, Appaloosas) have sold well in Europe; dude horses, in Japan; and Thoroughbreds and Arabians, in the Middle East.

With the chance for greater profit, however, comes the chance for greater marketing expenses and problems. In some cases, the language barrier will force you to learn the language or use a translator. You will need to research the customs of the country so you don't make any faux pas. Some foreign business practices preclude women transacting sales. All foreign sales will require greater sales expenses (shipping costs, agent's fee, etc.). There will be at least double the red tape regarding quarantines, health certificates, and money exchanges. You will need to take into account foreign holidays in all steps of the transaction. Foreign sales are more stressful to the horse (air travel, delays, quarantine, etc.), to say nothing of the stress it can cause you if you are thousands of miles away.

ESTABLISHING A VALUE AND PRICE FOR YOUR HORSE

We'd all like to own, train, or sell the perfect horse. The perfect horse is an ideal we use for comparison and evaluation and will probably never see. Sometimes in their enthusiasm owners overrate their horses in terms of conformation and ability, and inadvertently misrepresent them. Not every horse has the potential to go to a World Championship show or the Olympics.

An honest assessment of your horse's quality may best be done by an objective professional. You may learn that your horse has the conformation to compete in breed halter classes, or place in area reining competitions, or be appropriate for second level dressage movements. Conversely, you may be informed of detracting points that limit your horse's marketability. Receiving an informed opinion will help you represent your product honestly.

Try to price your horse realistically. Remember, his value is not based on what you paid for him or have invested in him financially or emotionally, but rather on what he is worth to someone else. Be honest about his level and potential and find out what people have recently spent for similar animals, those of similar age, sex, breed, level of training, and size. Some horses appreciate in value, some depreciate rapidly. If you buy a six-year-old gelding for $3,000, you could get as much or more for him at ten if he is sound and has just become more solid with the years. If you buy a five-figure two-year-old after a win at a futurity but the horse matures into just another horse, you will probably have difficulty recouping your investment. Establishing the value of foals is usually based on the stud fee plus travel, vet costs, and mare care to weaning. With a stud fee of $1,000 and using a cost of raising a foal to weaning at about $1,400, the value of a weaning foal would be about $2,400. Since an "average" weanling foal would likely command a price in the $500–$1,200 range, not the $2,400 range, it doesn't "pay" to raise average foals, but it can be profitable to raise exceptional foals that would bring the true value. When establishing the value on any of your horses, get several opinions if necessary. You can hire a well-respected, knowledgeable judge, trainer, horse auctioneer, or equine appraiser to help you establish your horse's price.

An equine appraiser can determine the horse's monetary value as of a specific date. This is the horse's fair market value. FMV involves costs or replacement value, market value, and a horse's future earning power. In order to determine FMV, the appraiser must be experienced, certified in horses, and must be an independent third party. His fee will be based on time and expenses.

When it might be beneficial to hire an appraiser:

- to establish a horse's fair market value
- to establish the value of a horse being donated, especially those over $5,000
- to establish value of a horse involved in insurance claims or damage suits
- to establish the value of a horse before an insurance policy is issued
- to help a seller establish and get his price
- to help a buyer make purchases

Determine your bottom price, then add 10 to 15 percent to it. Horse trading really hasn't changed in the regard that offers and counteroffers still are an expected part of the sale.

A horse's conformation and training exert the greatest influence on price. Good management and preparation, however, can increase a horse's chances of bringing full market value.

Chapter Ten

Marketing a Horse

If you are busy or inexperienced in the sale of horses or simply not able to locate a buyer, you may want to consider having a professional aid you in selling your horse. You can either use a private treaty agent or an auction sale company.

SELLING THROUGH AN AGENT OR AUCTION

Agents set up their sales arrangements many different ways but generally charge a flat fee and a percentage of the sale price of the horse. In addition, most agents require the horse to be boarded and in training at the agent's facility. In some cases you will receive a reduced price (horse's market value less agent's fee) for your horse, and you may need to invest money (for training and boarding) in order to sell your horse. But having your horse at the agent's barn makes it most efficient for the horse to be prepared and presented in a professional manner to prospective buyers. For a fee, an agent does all the advertising, promotion, and phone, mail, and video follow-up to queries. The agent is also responsible for the grooming, training, showing, and presentation of the horse. Most agents network with other agents, often across the country, so a horse may get wide exposure.

An agent might simply be a respected trainer with whom you have done business previously, or he or she might be an instructor. If you need to locate an agent, either ask for local recommendations or read breed and association publications. Many sales agents advertise, "Let us sell your horse for you." If possible, visit the agent so you can get a feel for his or her manner and view the facilities. Ask yourself how you would feel arriving at these facilities and dealing with the agent if you were a buyer. The great thing about dealing with an honest, respected sales agent is that you have very minimal time investment in the sales effort.

Selling a horse through an auction has its pros and cons. Auctions are less time-consuming than private treaty sales because all the buyers are in one place at one time and the horse sells. Still, you will need to invest the time and money to prepare the horse for the auction. The horse must be fit, well groomed, and well trained. Some auctions require horses over two or three years of age to be ridden in the sales ring. Many auctions have requirements that must be met by the horse and the consignor. (See sidebar.)

The fees involved in selling a horse at auction vary greatly. Most charge a nonrefundable consignment fee. If the horse does not sell (you exercise your right to reject the highest bid and repurchase the horse), the consignment fee compensates the auction company for the horse's listing in the catalog, the stall space at the sale, and the exposure it received in the sale ring. In addition to the consignment fee, there will be a commission charged on the sale price of the horse. This will vary from 5 to 15 percent depending on the circumstances. Averages range from 7 to 10 percent. Some small sales (less expensive horses) charge only a consignment fee. Some sales charge only a commission. The charge of both a consignment fee plus a commission is most common. Some sales stipulate a consignment fee plus either a commission (a percentage) or a dollar amount, whichever is greater. (Example: $275 consignment plus 8 percent commission or $150, whichever is greater.)

SAMPLE TERMS AND CONDITIONS TO BE CONSIDERED BEFORE CONSIGNING A HORSE TO AN AUCTION

- Horse must be registered and papers in order.
- Consignor must have absolute title to horse.
- Consignment fee, registration papers, and transfer must accompany application.
- Sale screening committee will select horses for the sale and reserves the right to reject any applicant.
- After a horse has been accepted and consigned, the seller agrees not to sell the horse through private treaty. If horse is withdrawn from the sale, a withdrawal fee will be charged in addition to the consignment fee.
- Horse must have current (30–180 days) negative Coggins test.

- Horse must be HYPP negative.
- Horse must have health certificate dated less than 10 days from the sale.
- Consignor must furnish own feed and bedding and care for the horse until sold.
- Consignor must furnish a halter and lead rope.
- All responsibilities and guarantees lie solely between buyer and consignor.
- A recorded video or audio tape will be made of the sale to determine what announcements or claims were made during the sale.
- Sales management will settle with consignor not later than 10 banking days after the sale.
- Consignor will pay transfer fee.
- Consignor releases sales management from all responsibilities, liabilities, obligations, claims, law suits, or legal proceedings arising from the sale of this horse.
- A drawing for sales order will be held by the sales management company.
- Consignor must notify sales management if horse has been on medication or drugs within 30 days of the sale.
- If a consignor wishes to repurchase the horse to *no sale* the horse, it is the sole responsibility of the consignor (or his agent) to be present to do the bidding.

ADVERTISING

Bulletin boards   The simplest, and least expensive form of advertising is the use of bulletin boards. You can pin your ads on boards at your feed store, tack store, and farm supply store. You may even wish to include bulletin boards at supermarkets, laundromats, and gas stations. One of the best kind of ads is a flattering color photo of the horse, with a simple message, and take-home phone number and other information for interested parties. The description of your horse should include the age, sex, size, color, breed, and price. Be sure the height is accurate by using a measuring stick. Your ad can also describe the personality and training level of the horse. For example:

FOR SALE Bright sorrel Quarter Horse gelding. Shown in 4–H western classes. Quiet and kind. 15 hands 15 years $1500. Call George Green at 221–1500.

Farm sign   If your farm is located on a highway and you don't mind people dropping in unexpectedly, a neat, easy-to-read sign might draw a buyer your way. However, don't prop up an old car hood in the pasture and paint

HORSE 4 SALE

on it with a cloth daubed in paint as I have seen some do! I admit such a sign got my attention, but I just didn't want to look at the kind of horse that was behind that car hood! Instead, neatly paint a simple message in large letters:

FOR SALE

ENDURANCE MARE

221–1616

OR DRIVE IN

Classified ads   Classified ads will increase the cost of selling your horse, and a single ad will rarely do the trick. Sales strategy indicates that keeping a well-written ad running continuously is necessary if you hope to sell your horse. Running a single ad is like throwing away money. Compare costs and readership profiles of appropriate advertising mediums: your local newspaper, the nearest city paper, a shopper's guide, a horse shopper's guide, various riding club newsletters, and the classified sections of various regional and national horse publications. Then pare your ad down to bare bones while still retaining its clarity and accuracy.

Direct mail flyers   If you have a highly targeted list of people who might be interested in buying your horse, it might be a good investment to design a simple flyer, a fact sheet on your horse. The flyer can also be sent as a self-mailer, a folded sheet with address on one blank side rather than using an envelope. (Self-mailers have a reputation for getting mutilated in automated post office equipment, especially if you use staples to seal the edges.) The same flyer might be useful on bulletin boards as well.

Word of mouth   More horse selling is done by word of mouth than any other way. In order for this method to work for you, you must have a circle of personal and business acquaintances who know your name and how to contact you. Then, each time you buy feed, tack, or something at your hardware store, you mention you have a horse for sale. Obviously, if you frequent a stable regularly for boarding or lessons, the people there would be natural connections for the sale of your horse.

Public appearances   Every time you or your horse appear in public, it can serve as a means to encourage or deter people from contacting you about a horse that might be for sale. If you participate in community equine activities as a volunteer (show help, trail restoration crew, handicapped riding program, etc.), use the networking benefits to let people know you have a horse for sale. If you take lessons on the horse that is for sale (and the horse does well in his lessons!), be sure to let everyone at the facility know that he is for sale. If you are a more involved rider, you know that every time you participate in a clinic, demonstration, parade, or horse show (even if you are riding a different horse from the one you have for sale), you are involved in a critical form of advertising. If you have your own stable, you might want to consider having an open house to familiarize the community with the services you offer as well as the horse(s) you have for sale. You may even wish to consider hats, shirts, or jackets with your farm name for you and your employees.

Publicity Free publicity can help you sell a horse if you plan ahead. If you are ever contacted by a local publication that wants to do a feature story on your business, even though it might not be horse-related, mention in the interview that you do occasionally sell horses. If your business is ag-related, send press releases to local publications whenever you have noteworthy news. Name recognition will help when it comes time for you to sell a horse.

Display ads Printed ads larger than classifieds are costly but often get the attention necessary to attract a buyer for more expensive horses. Display ads are available in many local general news and ag-related publications as well as in over 300 equine publications in the United States. It is important to target your buyer and choose the appropriate publication. Request an ad kit (or a media kit), which should contain a sample copy of the publication, ad rate card, and a fact sheet of reader demographics such as age, income, family size, occupation, geographic area, and types of goods and services used.

For larger ads, it will be beneficial for you to calculate the CPM (cost per thousand readers) for the magazines you are considering advertising in. Divide the cost of the ad by the circulation and multiply by 11,000. If the ad costs $500 and the magazine has a 10,000-reader circulation, the CPM is $50, which can also be expressed as 5 cents per reader. The cost of a display ad depends on the magazine, whether the ad will be in color or black and white, the size of the ad, the location of the ad, the number of times the ad is run, and whether the ad was placed by a professional ad agency in camera-ready form.

You will need to book space for your ad from one day to three months ahead of printing, depending on the publication. Newspapers operate on very tight deadlines. Monthly glossy color magazines usually require two to three months' lead time. Deadlines are critical, and if the ad is not there, not only will it not be printed in the issue, you might be liable for paying for (at least a percentage of) the space that was saved for it.

Display ads should look professional, but that is not to say you cannot design and lay the ad out yourself. A horse ad is most effective with a dominant, attention-getting photo. Photos are more effective in capturing a reader's attention than drawings. The copy of the ad should start out with a *headline,* which is a short phrase that states the single most important selling point of the horse and uses powerful, descriptive words that are unique but accurate. The *subhead* reinforces or explains the headline. It can be a longer phrase or a short sentence. The *body copy* provides necessary details. It is the longest portion of the copy (several phrases or sentences) but still should be concise. The *action instructions* tell the now interested prospective buyer how, where, and how much. The *summary* closes the ad by rewording the headline.

Avoid some of the most common pitfalls in self-designed (and some professionally designed!) ads by adhering to the following:

- Be sure to list the name of a person the reader should contact.
- List, as appropriate, the phone, fax, mailing address, location map.
- Indicate HORSE FOR SALE somewhere in the ad so it doesn't appear to be a promotional ad or a thank-you ad from a previous owner to a new owner.
- Use the price of the horse in the ad only if you think it is necessary to narrow the queries you get from potential buyers and you don't mind being locked into that price as the highest you can ask.
- Keep the ad simple. Focus on the horse for sale, and don't also expect the ad to effectively promote your horse-training business, boarding stable, etc.
- Use a white background with dark letters. Reverse contrast (white letters on black) reduces readership significantly.
- Consider running a display ad and a classified ad in the same magazine because some people only look at classified ads, assuming that big ads mean expensive horses and intimidating or snooty sellers.
- If selling a Quarter Horse, consider listing that he is HYPP negative if he has been tested.

The layout of the ad should result in a clear message with a focal point and graphics and copy that fit together. Don't be afraid to use white space, as it keeps things from being cluttered. The ad should be proofread very carefully several times by several people. It is very easy to pass over incorrect spellings and numbers, errors that sometimes make the ad totally useless to you as the seller.

Most magazines require that ads be *camera-ready*, which means ready to reproduce. You can print the copy with a computer and laser printer and paste the ad up yourself, or you can hire a professional ad agency to do it for you. Some magazines will use your copy and design a very simple ad for a variable charge.

ADVERTISING TERMINOLOGY

Bleed Ads with color, black, or a screen that extends all the way to the paper's edge.

Camera ready The state of an ad that is ready to be photographed for printing: typeset, laid out on an art board with all graphics and artwork complete and in specific dimensions to fit the ad space and publication it will be used in; a camera-ready ad is also called a *mechanical.*

Color separation Making four separate positives or negatives from a full-color photo so it can be reproduced in a publication.

Copy The words used in an advertisement.

CPM Cost per thousand; a way of measuring how many readers an ad will reach; often used to compare effectiveness of advertising in similar publications.

Display ad An ad other than a classified that uses graphics, various typefaces, headlines, white space (layout), and color.

Font Letters and numbers in a particular typeface and size.

Halftone A photograph converted to a series of black, gray, and white dots so it can be printed.

Mock-up A dummy or initial layout of an ad.

PMT or stat A high-quality reproduction (usually of a photo or art) that is ready for printing.

Screen A lighter shade of a color described by a percentage.

Photos Since photos are such a critical part of an ad, do not take their effect lightly and use the snapshot Aunt Gertie took of Lacey out in the pasture. Depending on the price of the horse, you might be better off hiring a professional photographer. If economics force you to try your hand at capturing your horse on film, you'll get best results using a 35mm single-lens reflex camera with a telephoto lens (100mm to 200mm) and standing fifty feet away from the horse. This will avoid most distortions. Shoot from a low point—some pros even lie on the ground to get a flattering view.

If you are going to run a black-and-white ad, use black-and-white film because color prints or slides used as black and white often suffer a loss of contrast when converted. If the shooting conditions are bright and the horse is still, use ISO (also referred to as ASA or DIN) 64, 100, or 200 film to get sharp, rich detail and good contrast. If the light is low or the horse is in motion, you will need to use a "faster" film, ISO 400–1000. This film will capture leg movement without blur but will result in a grainy photo, a fuzziness especially apparent in enlargements.

Be aware of the most common mistakes made in taking horse photos so that you

- choose the right film for the light conditions and action
- use a high-quality lens and learn to focus correctly
- be sure the background offers a good contrast with the horse
- select a simple background without such distractions as telephone poles, wires, fences, surprise trees, or farm equipment
- shoot from a low angle, using the sky as a background if necessary
- lie on the ground to get good foal photos
- stand the horse on level ground; don't have fences in the photo that aren't absolutely straight and tidy
- make sure the grass is short
- have the horse impeccably groomed and in excellent condition, not dimple fat or with ribs showing
- use a halter (or bridle) that fits well and is complimentary (color, style) to the horse
- are sure, if shooting a performance shot, that the rider is photogenic and dressed neatly and conservatively, so as not to draw attention away from the horse
- have plenty of fly spray on hand
- have attention-getters available (helpers, squeaky toys, bucket of grain, mirror, whip with plastic on end, etc.)
- shoot in the morning or late afternoon or you risk having shadows on the horse's legs and chest or the rider's face.

If you are after a conformation shot, generally the best shots are a side view or a 3/4 front view. For the side view, pose the horse with all four legs showing. The legs nearest the camera should be perpendicular to the ground. The legs farthest from the camera should be more under the horse's body: The farther hind foot is ahead of the closer hind and the farther front foot is behind the closer front. Shoot directly into the horse's heart girth.

For the 3/4 front view, move the hind foot that is farthest from the camera one or two inches ahead of the other hind. Move the front leg that is closest to the camera about an inch behind the other front. Then shoot square into the horse's shoulder.

A popular Quarter Horse shot is the 3/4 rear view to showcase the spectacular hindquarters. Arabian conformation shots often emphasize the head from a variety of angles.

After you have your proof prints in hand, be sure you have several horse people who are unfamiliar with your horse critique the photos honestly, telling

Photographs of Arabians often emphasize the head.

you how they make the horse look. If you consistently hear that the horse looks like he has a large head or a weak hindquarters, you should not use those photos. It might be time to enlist the aid of a professional photographer.

Response to your ads   When people respond to your ad by telephone, be sure you provide them with accurate and honest information. Have a detailed description of the horse and other important information near the phone. Keep a photocopy of important papers with the information. Be sure that everyone at the phone number you listed knows that you have a horse for sale and is willing to be helpful to callers.

If it seems like your horse would be appropriate for a caller, encourage him or her to come and check your horse. After all, it doesn't cost to look. You might mention to your caller that when horse shopping, it is a good idea to look at as many horses as possible.

If your ad covers a large geographical area, plan to have good photos or a videotape ready to send to interested parties. A videotape, like photos, must show your horse to advantage. He must be impeccably groomed and on model behavior. The background for photos and videos should be uncluttered, so the prospective buyer has a clear view of your horse. The person operating either the photo or video camera should be experienced and the results should be sharp. Remember, with videos, if a horse makes a mistake, the viewer may play that part of the tape over and over. A poor photo or video is worse than none at all.

Producing a video may greatly assist you in selling your horse. Prospective buyers will have the opportunity to see your horse at his best.

VIDEO AS A MARKETING TOOL

An effective video captures a horse at his best. It showcases his best features and talents. The content of such a tape should cover the horse's conformation, movement, and performance yet not be longer than five or ten minutes. At larger competitions, there will be at least one professional video company at work from whom you can order footage of your horse. This might be a valuable addition to footage shot at the horse's home barn.

Use of Videos in Selling Horses

In a classified or display ad for a private treaty sale, if you include the word VIDEO in the ad (and have a good one to send), many more people will respond to your ad because they will be able to further consider your horse without driving. Private treaty sales tapes should run five to ten minutes or longer, especially if they contain competition shots.

If your horse is to be sold at a large sale, playing a video of the horse's performance outside of his stall really draws attention. This is an excellent marketing device for events that require specialized equipment such as jumping, specialized footing such as reining, or cattle such as roping, cutting, team penning, etc. You can showcase a horse's skills from previous competitions or work at home. There are several companies that make small color TVs with video players built in. All you need at the sale is a table and an extension cord. Some auctions play tapes for the audience prior to selling a horse. Keep auction tapes short and sweet, about two to three minutes. Be sure the horse's lot number is on the tape.

If your horse is to be listed with a broker or agent, have a video ready to send to interested parties. Some brokers do the videotaping for you and some require that you do it. (See "Some Things to Consider Including in a Video Action Script," pp. 167–168.) Most agents do not want your name, address, or phone number on the tape, and in some instances they even want the horse's name and registration number omitted. This is because the agent wants all inquiries and the eventual commission to come to him or her.

The Making of a Video

If you plan to produce your own video, consider the following requirements for a high-quality video and you'll probably be scurrying to hire a professional:

- Make a specific shooting plan (storyboard) before you begin (see box).
- Use a high-quality camera such as a Hi 8 or Super VHS to get a quality master that you can make copies from.
- Use a tripod to eliminate shaking and fuzziness. Tripods are available for under $50. Or position yourself firmly against a fence, tree, building, or car.
- For conformation shots, be still and steady with a tripod, or set the camera on a solid object.
- To get good results, you must be a competent camera operator, familiar and experienced with the equipment.
- Learn to pan (follow the horse's action), keeping the entire horse in the frame, with a little space ahead of the horse (this is called *leading the action*).

- Shoot in good light. Sunny outdoor shots are the best, but never shoot into the sun or you will get a silhouette. If you shoot at midday or on an overcast day, you will not have to worry about shooting into the sun.
- If you are shooting indoors, much artificial light must be provided.
- The raw footage you get must be selected and edited. You can do some editing within the camera, more by using your camera and VCR, and even a better job with an edit controller. Inexpensive home model controllers cost $200.
- A narration should be dubbed over the final edited tape. This can be done with most camcorders.
- Music can be added as background and filler to tie things together.
- The grooming and turnout of the horse and handler must be appropriate in terms of style, color, etc. Red and orange tend to bleed. White tends to be too bright.
- The background must not distract from the horse and his performance.

Sample Shooting Plan

Length of time	*Action*	*Where*
30 seconds	Opening: tempi lead changes, pirouette	In competition
1 minute	Conformation shots	At home
1 minute	Traveling in-hand	At home
6 minutes	Riding entire Grand Prix test	At home
30 seconds	Head shot, pleasant expression or in-hand personality shot with owner	At home

Generation loss   Beware of generation loss, which is a diminishing of quality with each subsequent copy you make. For example, the original tape of raw footage (source tape) in your camera is the first generation. If you edit the footage onto another tape, the edited version (master) is now second generation. You'll want to retain the edited master, so when you make copies to send out, they would be third generation. If you plan what you want your tape to contain and edit as you film, right in your camera, then dub the sound onto the first-generation master, the copies you send out will be a richer, sharper second-generation copy. If you do not have the capacity to make copies, look in the Yellow Pages for companies that do.

Narration

The narration should be written out and include pertinent information, such as:

- The horse's name
- Pedigree
- Age, sex, height, weight
- How long you have owned him
- Background of the horse
- Type of tack used
- Level of training and performance
- Your name, address, and phone number
- Price of the horse

Practice reading the narration several times as you watch your finished video, and make notes so you know where to pause or speed up to keep the spoken words in sync with the action. Then dub the narration onto the master tape.

SOME THINGS TO CONSIDER INCLUDING IN A VIDEO ACTION SCRIPT

- Show ring performances
- Conformations shots
    Profile from each side
    Front view, from the chest down (head gets distorted)
    Rear view, entire hindquarters
    Closeup of head, from the side that is more flattering
    Closeup of legs
- Manners
    Catch
    Tied
    Fly spray
    Clip
    Bathe
    Shoe
    Load in trailer
    Blanket

Saddle

Bridle

Lead near or over obstacles

Longe

Drive

Mount

Ride (see Movement)

- Movement

    In-hand at a walk and trot—to and from the camera

    In-hand at a walk and trot—profile to the camera

    All gaits free in a round pen or arena

    All gaits ridden

    Specialized maneuvers (if you are selling a roping horse, the majority of the tape should focus on roping runs, not walk, trot, canter; if you are selling a youth horse, emphasize safety, dependability, at all gaits and in various settings; if you are selling a young horse, emphasize manners and conformation, possibly movement depending on age)

    Being ridden out of the arena

VIDEO NO-NOS

- No halters on free horses
- No screaming horses on the soundtrack
- No junk in the background
- No shooting into the sun
- No poor riders
- No sloppy handlers
- No dusty arenas
- No horse kicking while being longed
- No free longeing (or chasing a horse around) in a large arena (longeing free in a round pen is all right)
- No clucking or baby talk on the soundtrack

When you get a request for a copy of the video, send the video and a self-addressed return mailer or a self-addressed label to be used over the old mailing label. Whether you supply return postage is up to you. If you tell the person requesting the video that he or she will have to pay for its return, it may eliminate those folks who are merely curious, not serious. These people will decline having you send the tape in the first place, or they may request it and then not send it back at all. However, you might also discourage a serious buyer who just doesn't like to deal with the minor hassle of returning a tape. Ideally, the tape will generate enough interest that the party will come to look at the horse in person and can return the tape to you at that time, or better yet, buy the horse and keep the tape! If you can afford it, provide a self-addressed, stamped return mailer to make it convenient for the prospective buyer and to ensure that you will get your tape back.

Include a fact sheet with all videos you send out. The fact sheet should be dated and include:

- Your name, address, phone (best hours to reach you), fax
- Horse's name, birth date (not age, as changes will show the horse has been on the market for a long time!), sex, height, weight, color, markings
- Horse's pedigree
- Horse's training
- Horse's accomplishments
- Price

Chapter Eleven

Presentation of a Horse for Sale

When a buyer makes an effort to travel to your place to take a look at a horse you have for sale, prepare for the visit and show the horse to his best advantage. The physical appearance of you, your facilities, and your horse make a distinct and lasting impression on a prospective buyer.

The horse's appearance Proper nutrition, deworming, and exercise have the biggest effect on a horse's overall health picture. The horse's eye and coat should be bright. His hair should be smooth, his attitude alert. No amount of bathing and coat conditioner can substitute for long-term good management. Although a horse's bloom comes from continuous good health, certain "last-minute" things can be done to enhance your horse's outward appearance.

If you are showing a horse for sale in the winter, you basically have two choices: Show the horse in a full winter coat or give him a very neat trace or body clip. Refer to the appendix for books that explain how to do this. If you are showing a broodmare or a very young horse, it is acceptable to show the horse more *au natural* than you would a performance horse.

Clip your horse according to breed standards and intended use. Be sure you know what is acceptable. Clipping the legs, fetlocks, and coronet very short might look fine to a halter showman but may make the horse appear weak and vulnerable to a prospective endurance rider. Clipping ears, whiskers, and eyelashes may turn a customer right on or off, depending on their intended use for the horse.

The bridle path should be freshly clipped but not too far down the horse's neck. If you are uncertain what is appropriate for your horse's breed or type, only

A diamond in the rough coming off winter pasture.

The same horse after a bath, tail let-down, and overall trim.

clip two or three inches from the poll rearward. For example, the extremely long bridle path of the Arabian would be inappropriate for the hunter.

Mane and tail lengths and styles vary between breeds and sometimes for each performance event. For example, Quarter Horses used for roping often have tails ending just below the hocks and roached or very short manes. Quarter Horses used for reining, however, are usually shown with a full-length mane and a tail that ends just above the ground. If you are selling your horse for a certain niche, prepare his mane and tail that way. But if he has versatile uses, be on the safe side and leave his mane and tail as long as possible. That way the new owner can visualize trimming and shaping the mane and tail to his or her preference. But be

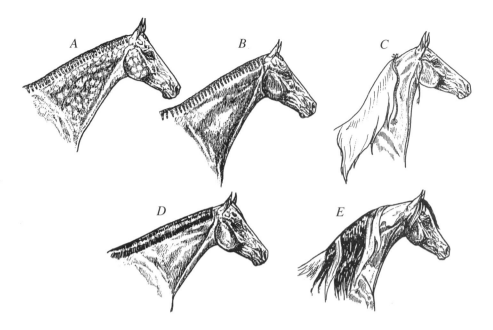

Mane Styles. A: dressage B: hunter C: show D: stock E: pleasure or reining
From Hill, From the Center of the Ring.

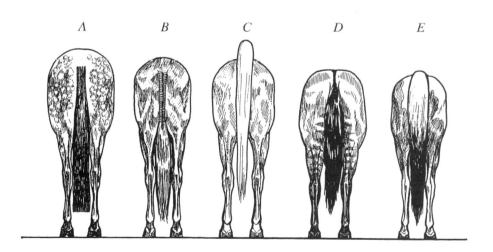

Tail Styles. A: dressage B: hunter C: show D: stock E: pleasure or reining
From Hill, From the Center of the Ring.

sure the mane and tail are squeaky clean and silky soft and well brushed. All manes should be trained to lie on one side of the neck. Some events specify the right side. You can use mane banding or mane tamers to help with this task.

Proper shoeing is critical to the health and overall appearance of the horse. Nail clinches should be tight; the hoof should be shod at the correct angle; there should be room for expansion left at the quarters. The shoe should be of a size that provides adequate support for the leg. Keeping your horse on a regular shoeing schedule ensures he will look good *whenever* someone comes to see him. Before you show your horse, pick the hooves and wipe the hoof wall with a damp cloth. You can apply a hoof sealer that dries quickly and with a hard finish. Don't put hoof dressing on just before a buyer looks at the horse, as the greasy dressing will pick up dirt and look bad.

Wipe your horse's eyes and nostrils for that finished look. Put a sheet on your bathed or well-brushed horse and put him in a freshly bedded stall until the prospective buyers arrive.

The handler's appearance   The handler's (and owner's) appearance and manner are more important than you probably realize. During the prospective buyer's visit, he or she might be positively identifying with the handler or owner, thinking subconsciously, "If I own this horse, I will be like this person." On the other hand, if a buyer receives a negative image from the owner, he might be thinking, "I wouldn't be caught dead buying a horse that was owned by someone like that!"

Work on your horse's weak points, because they will be sure to surface when a buyer is present.

The handler or rider should be neat, clean, and dressed conservatively so as not to draw attention away from the horse.

The facilities   The barn and outside pens should be immaculate. The arena should be freshly dragged. Fences and gates should be in safe operation and maintenance. There should be no manure or debris lying around. Horses that are in view should be clean, and if wearing blankets, these should not appear to be leftovers from World War II. Be aware of the presence of flies. If they are particularly pesky, spray horses and facilities before the buyer's arrival.

Manners   A horse should be safe and cooperative when he is handled. Manners in the stall, in-hand, and in preparation for riding are important considerations to a prospective buyer. Refer to chapter 5. Who would want to buy a horse that is sullen in the cross-ties or wrestles you for a hind foot or has a viselike jaw when being bridled? Work on your horse's weak points before you put a horse up for sale, because you can be sure a buyer will ask you to demonstrate the very thing you hope to avoid! The time for training is not with a buyer looking on. You should allow a buyer to observe your horse in a variety of settings and possibly to be involved in the handling, grooming, and tacking of your horse if he or she

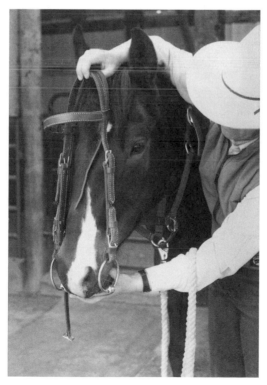

Be sure your horse is well-mannered for bridling as this is one area of particular problem during a buyer exam.

requests it. If a horse has a dangerous bad habit, bring it to the attention of a prospective buyer and price the horse accordingly.

Getting a fix on the buyer's wants and needs   When a prospective buyer phones or visits, greet her warmly and make her feel her call or visit is welcome. Listen carefully to everything the buyer says and take notes. Her comments will be a valuable reference later. Don't do a lot of irrelevant talking but answer all of her questions honestly and thoroughly. Ask her questions to pinpoint what she is looking for. The answers will also tell you if she is a serious buyer and appropriate for your horse.

- Do you have horses now?
- Do you keep them at home?
- What do you use them for?
- Who will ride this horse?
- Do you have children?
- Do you show?
- What will you use this horse for?

The above questions will likely lead to many others. By the time you finish talking, you will have a good idea of her price range, the type and quality of horse she is looking for, and if you have one that fits her bill. I don't think it is polite or ethical for a seller to ask a buyer what the top dollar is that they can spend because it just sounds like a setup. I'd rather listen to what the buyer says as we talk and then say, "I have a three-year-old gelding for $6,500. He is _____ (vital statistics). Does he sound like he might work for you?" The buyer's response will tell you if the price range is acceptable. As you work with a buyer, don't focus on a one-time sale. It is better to tell a buyer that you don't have anything suitable at this time rather than trying to talk her into a horse that is inappropriate. That buyer, or her friends, may come to you in the future because of your honesty.

Customer selection   It is less time-consuming, less risky, and less disappointing if you use a customer selection process when you sell horses. When you run an ad, many of the phone calls could be from curious parties rather than serious buyers. Often people with no intention of ever looking at a horse respond to ads to ask a price. If you let the person on the other end of the phone carry the conversation, you will soon learn why they have called. You can give them the information they are after and get off the phone, minimizing your time expenditure. This will save your enthusiasm for legitimate inquiries. The same goes for showing horses. Some folks arrive unannounced and want to see every horse on the place. It is much better if you have a series of questions you ask a buyer to pre-qualify him or her before you head out to the barn to begin showing horses or you could be wasting your time. I get the feeling that some folks go out horse shopping like they would mall hopping or garage sale hunting. It is a recreational activity. On the other hand, serious buyers will show the obvious signs of anticipation, eagerness, and great interest in what you have for sale.

You will be subject to less liability if you deal with good folks that have a solid commitment to owning horses. If you make a marginal sale (you had to talk them into it or offer them a generous contract sale) you shouldn't be surprised if the buyer skips payment or doesn't care for the horse properly. Also, taking the time to select the best buyer for your horse also results in less follow-up or chance of return due to breach of warranty.

Showing a horse to a buyer   As you show your horse to a buyer, be honest, courteous, and informative. Refer to chapters 4, 5, and 6. First show the horse to the buyer in a halter and lead line. Stand the horse in a level, well-lighted place where the buyer can get around on all sides of the horse and can stand back and get a good view. An aisle of a barn is often not wide enough to get back for a really good profile view.

It's customary to then demonstrate the horse's movement in-hand at a walk and a trot in a straight line. The buyer might want to watch the horse from the front and rear as well as from the side. You may have to trot the horse several times back and forth to satisfy a discerning buyer.

Then you might be asked to either turn the horse loose or work him on a longe line. Buyers concerned with natural movement and charisma might prefer to see

Ride the horse for the buyer to warm the horse up and demonstrate the horse's capabilities.

the horse exercise freely. Others might prefer to see the horse's frame and carriage during longeing, his style of movement and the methods of your ground training. Longeing is a convenient warmup for riding, tuning the horse to the aids, and burning off a little energy.

Whether you are demonstrating ground work or mounted work, be sure your horse is reliable and sound. Indicate to a buyer any habits that a horse has that may cause trouble. It is best if a horse is in regular work when shown to a prospective buyer. When a horse is fit and ridden daily, his responses tend to be more dependable than if he were just pulled out of a pasture.

You or your agent should ride the horse first to demonstrate his capabilities. Try to approach it as a demonstration rather than a training session. If you get into a long, repetitive drilling, the buyer may lose interest. Instead, perform the things the horse knows well.

LIABILITY DURING THE TEST RIDE

If you are not a professional horseman, your homeowner's liability policy should cover you in the event a rider gets hurt while test-riding a horse you have for sale. Be sure to check with your insurance agent on this coverage.

If you are a professional, you probably have a business liability policy that would cover you in case of a mishap. However, a good number of states have recently passed legislation stating that equine professionals are *not* responsible for accident or death to riders due to the inherent risk of equine activities. In those states, an equine professional is usually required to post a sign stating the rider's responsibility. In many cases it is advisable to have all riders sign an acknowledgment and release of liability. Trial rides are potentially risky and should always be preceded by a discussion between seller and buyer of the risks involved and the use of safety equipment and safe horse handling techniques.

Then, if the buyer wishes to try the horse, assist him or her in whatever way you can. Some buyers bring a personal saddle for the test ride. If it will properly fit the horse, help with the adjustments and offer to hold the horse for mounting. While the buyer is becoming accustomed to the horse, you might want to chat to relax them both or leave them to their work in silence. Be aware of the urge to help verbally. This can be greatly appreciated or resented. Try to get a feel for what the potential buyer would prefer.

You can inadvertently insult someone's riding abilities by claiming with surprise that your horse has "never done that before!" If you are overly defensive about your horse, it may appear as though you are blaming the rider for an error. It is best to accept the responsibility yourself for the horse's behavior, since you

If the buyer wants to ride, assist the buyer in mounting by holding the reins.

Help the buyer get situated.

Give the buyer and the horse time to relax by talking about the horse's training.

Let the buyer proceed at her own pace.

Even if the horse does not perform as well as you know she can, resist the urge to say so or to give the buyer a lesson.

As the test ride comes to an end, ask the buyer, "Do you think she will work for you?"

are the trainer/owner. Perhaps you have made an error in judgment as to the horse's suitability. A good intermediate horse may *not* be a good beginning horse.

After the trial ride, answer all questions honestly and thoroughly. Beware of providing too many anecdotes. Not only can storytelling be time-consuming, but it can backfire on you. What might sound very cute to you might sound irresponsible to the prospective buyer. As the buyer prepares to leave, give her something to remind her of your horse. It can be a photo of the horse with your name and phone number on the back, an information sheet about the horse, a business card, or a paper with some of the pertinent information on it.

Things That Kill a Sale

- Suspicious behavior: whispering, incomplete answers, blushing, stammering
- Not pointing out obvious problems
- Evasive answers to buyer's legitimate questions
- Finding out that a seller lied about something that might be very insignificant but leads the buyer to not trust the seller's word
- Antagonism between the seller and the veterinarian
- Antagonism between the seller and the buyer's trainer or agent
- Unfriendliness/coldness/snootiness
- Last-minute surprises
- Too much chitchat
- Making unrealistic predictions for the horse
- Saying the wrong thing ("This horse should mature to 16.2," when the buyer was hoping he'd stay more like 15.2)
- Being very opinionated about something and alienating the buyer (the use of bute; Impressive bloodlines in the Quarter Horse breed; feeding treats to horses)
- Wasting time showing the buyer dogs, other buildings, other horses, family photos
- Trying to demonstrate something the horse doesn't know well: crossing a bridge; jumping an oxer, performing flying changes
- Horse being "off"
- Paperwork not in order
- Sloppy, untidy appearance of horse, facilities, or handler.
- Annoying distractions such as phone calls, noisy children, barking dogs.

THINGS THAT MAKE A SALE

- Being honest. Honesty is not just the best policy, it is the only policy!
- Being open about a horse's problems
- Showing the buyer only one or two horses
- Asking the buyer, "Do you think he will work for you?"
- Presenting a clean, well-groomed, fit horse
- Letting the buyer have some "hands-on" time
- Setting a realistic value on a horse
- Being willing to negotiate in some way.
- Allowing the buyer to conduct a thorough exam performed by her farrier and veterinarian.

Be sure to make it convenient for the buyer to have a veterinarian and farrier examine the horse.

Chapter Twelve

---·---

Paperwork and Legalities
for the Seller

If you are selling a horse, be sure you have all the paperwork in order to satisfy the legal aspects of the transaction.

Information sheet Put together an information sheet for prospective buyers that provides answers to questions they may have when they're home "thinking it over." Include all of the horse's vital statistics: name, registration number, birth date, height, weight, color and markings, tattoos or brands, and performance titles, designations, or points. Also list briefly important health information such as: breeding records, major illnesses or injuries, vaccination and deworming records, farrier's records, and test results (Coggins, HYPP, etc.). Learn what the current health paper requirements are for the state the horse resides in as well as the one(s) he will be transported through and to. The seller will likely ask you to provide the necessary health certificate required for legal transport. (See appendix for listing by state).

Have copies of your horse's registration papers and pedigree to send home with interested buyers. That way, a buyer doesn't have to commit to memory the horse's lineage as you recite it but can refer to it later. Photos are an inexpensive way to remind your customers what you have for sale and can be included with the copy of the pedigree. Be sure the horse is flattered, that the image is sharp, clear, and large. It is counterproductive to use anything but a high-quality photo (see chapter 10).

Transfer of ownership   First of all, the registration papers must be in your name if you are the current owner. If a previous transfer of ownership was not registered with the breed association, it could make the current sales transaction sticky. It would be like you trying to sell a car in San Clemente, but the title is still in Joe Brown's name, and he lived in Buffalo a while back but is now deceased. This type of situation pops up quite frequently when horses change hands.

Each breed association has its own specific rules on the transfer of ownership. Often the seller is responsible for sending in the correctly completed transfer form, the transfer fee, and the horse's current (original) registration papers. The time to find out about the required regulations is well ahead of the day you sell the horse.

As soon as the purchase contract or transfer form is signed by the seller and the name of the buyer is entered as new owner, in most instances the risk of loss passes from the seller to the buyer. That's why a buyer can "legally" take possession of a horse before he or she actually receives *title* (the return of the papers from the breed association). In certain transactions, instead of relying solely on this inference, it might be wise to state in the purchase agreement exactly when the risk of loss is transferred.

When selling, be sure you make it clear to the buyer when risk of loss passes.

Unregistered horses, those with no official papers, can be sold with or without paperwork. Inexpensive horses often change hands without a sales contract. But every transaction should be at least documented with a bill of sale.

Many states require a brand inspection each time a horse is sold or purchased. The state livestock boards are charged with protecting livestock owners. They certify that the seller or shipper is the legal owner prior to issuing a brand certificate, so usually inspection is required at the point of origin. In states with brand boards, inspection is required on *all horses*, whether or not the horse is registered or branded. All horses being transported within and outside the state of origin must have a brand inspection and current health certificate (contact a local veterinarian or the state veterinarian for current information or see the appendix). If you are selling or buying in a state that does not have an inspection law and therefore you cannot obtain a certified inspection, be sure you obtain a bill of sale and health certificate.

SAMPLE BILL OF SALE

On July 1, 1999 Bea Rider (Buyer) of 1616 Hummingbird Lane, Sea View, South Carolina, paid Seventy five hundred dollars to Horace Poor (Seller) for the following horse: Ben Dickens, 6-year-old Selle Francais/Quarter Horse gelding (no papers), 16.2 hands, 1,250 pounds, sorrel with four white socks, star, strip, and snip. I, Horace Poor, am the lawful owner of the horse and have the right to sell him.

Signature of Seller _____

Name of Seller _____

Address _____

_____

Signature of Buyer _____

Signature of Witness (optional)_____

Installment sales Sometimes in order to entice or accommodate a buyer, you might want to offer a horse for sale on an installment contract, that is, the buyer would take possession of the horse after giving you a down payment and signing an installment payment agreement. If you are willing to offer such terms to a buyer, draft a contract that would suit you. Include such pertinent information as the amount of the down payment, the amount of the balance, and how and exactly when it will be paid (the number, amount, and frequency of payments to follow), the policy for late payments, default conditions, and insurance requirements until payoff. You can follow a standard loan contract from your bank or office supply store. See the appendix for the names of books that might be helpful.

When designing your contract, be sure you address:

- whether the buyer will pay interest. If a $1,000 horse is sold for a $500 down payment and two $250 payments two and four months after the sale, the seller may very well not charge interest. However, if an $8,000 horse is sold for a $2,000 down payment and monthly payments over two years, there very likely will be interest. All states have laws regulating the legal amount of interest that nonlending institutions can assess.
- what happens when a payment is late. Somewhere in the agreement there should be a statement related to the recourse for late payments. An extra charge (the amount or percentage specified) might be added to the payment or the horse might be repossessed after a certain number of late payments. A provision can be added stating that all payments made on a horse before the repossession are forfeited to the seller.
- who is responsible for selecting and paying for the insurance policy. Usually the seller selects the policy; the buyer pays for it.
- whether the insurance proceeds should be paid to the buyer or seller. The contract should be structured accordingly.
- whether the seller requires any specific care for the horse during the time of installment payments and what recourse the seller has if the buyer is not caring for the horse in the prescribed manner.
- whether the buyer is restricted from doing certain things with the horse (such as showing, certain types of strenuous riding, or training) or from hauling the horse out of the area until the purchase price is paid in full.

Payments are made on a predetermined schedule. The seller legally owns the horse until the last payment is made. Typically, at the time of the last payment, the registration papers and other identification papers are signed over to the new owner. Sometimes the buyer may obtain the papers before the last payment, but the seller holds a transfer form presigned by the buyer.

SAMPLE PURCHASE AND INSTALLMENT AGREEMENT

This agreement is made between Betty Buyer and Sally Seller for the purchase and sale of the horse described below on the following terms and conditions of sale.

Horse: Zoomerang, AQHA #16161616, foaled 6–16–86, bay mare with no white markings.

The seller agrees to sell the horse and the buyer agrees to buy the horse for the total sum of $_____. A down payment of $ _____is due by _____. The balance of $ _____shall be paid by buyer over _____ months at the rate of $ _____ per month. The first payment is due _____ and on the _____of each month thereafter. There will be no interest if the balance is paid by _____. If the total sum is not paid by _____, the seller reserves the right to either add _____% interest per month to the unpaid balance or foreclose on her Security Interest in any manner provided by law.

Payments over ____ days late will require a $ _____ late charge. Should the buyer fail to make _____ payments, the seller has the option to declare the balance of the note then owing to be due and payable.

To secure the payments, the seller retains the registration papers until the horse is paid in full. At that time, seller will execute appropriate transfer of ownership documents required by the breed registry.

The buyer agrees to keep the horse at Lofty Acres and will keep the horse in good health and free from disease by providing adequate feed, shelter, veterinary and farrier care.

The seller retains the right to inspect the horse at any reasonable hour with or without notice.

A veterinary pre-purchase examination constitutes acceptance by the buyer of the horse's soundness and health and any disease or unsoundness occurring after the date of this agreement is the buyer's responsibility. THE SELLER MAKES NO EXPRESS OR IMPLIED WARRANTIES OF THE HORSE BEING SOLD. [*Note: The previous statement must be conspicuous and in specific language per your state's UCC laws.*]

Should the buyer default in any terms of this agreement, the seller may foreclose on her Security Interest in any manner provided by law.

The seller warrants that she has good clear title to the horse and that the title is free of all liens and encumbrances.

The buyer agrees to carry full mortality insurance on the horse for the duration of this agreement. The seller and buyer will both be listed as loss payees, and in the event of the horse's death, the seller will be paid the balance due from insurance proceeds.

Death, injury, or incapacitation of the horse shall not relieve the buyer of her obligation to pay the purchase price as and when due.

The buyer agrees not to sell, lease, or otherwise encumber the horse without written permission of the seller until the horse is paid for in full.

Executed on _____, 19___ at City, State.

Seller's signature _____

Seller's name _____

Address _____

_____

Buyer's signature _____

Buyer's name _____

Address _____

_____

Notary Public (optional)

Note: This is only a sample. If you sell horses regularly, it would be a wise investment to develop a standard form in consultation with your attorney. If you are a buyer, it might be wise to consult with an attorney before signing a contract. For example, in order to secure the debt, the language used must be proper and a financing statement might need to be filed in accordance with your state's version of Article 9 of the Uniform Commercial Code. A financing statement (often called Uniform Commercial Code Form No. 1), once filed, becomes public record and the buyer's other creditors will have notice of your Security Interest in the horse. You will have priority over any of the buyer's other creditors who otherwise might try to possess the horse in settlement of their claims against the buyer.

Payment   Whether you are selling your horse for a full cash price or on installment, payment by the buyer can be made several ways. Ahead of time, decide which means of payment you will accept. If a buyer wants to use cash, be sure to issue him or her a receipt. Since a money order is basically just like cash, there should be no problems associated with accepting a money order, but generally the issuing limit is about $1,000.

Checks can be of several varieties. A *cashier's check* (also called a *certified check*) is the most desirable, as it is guaranteed money. The institution issuing a cashier's check has verified funds and guarantees the funds. The person "buying" the cashier's check cannot give the payee the check and then stop payment on the check. In addition, there are no holds on the check; it can be cashed or deposited and funds used immediately.

A *bank draft* is similar to a cashier's check but will vary from bank to bank. Usually the funds are verified before the draft is issued, but a bank draft does not bear the guarantee stamp as a cashier's check does. Both cashier's checks and bank drafts are large-format business checks made out to a specific party for a specific amount.

Personal and small business (stable, farm) checks are not guaranteed. It would be unwise to accept a personal check from someone you didn't know and sign over the title to your horse. If you call the bank listed on the check, and give them the account number, name, and amount of the check, they will tell you if there are funds available for the check to clear at that moment. However, there is no guarantee that the funds will be there when you deposit the check. Therefore, a cashier's check or bank draft is your best bet. If a personal check is the only option, you should retain possession of the horse and/or paperwork until the check clears your bank.

Warranties   A seller must be able to warrant that the title to the horse is good and that he has the right to sell the horse and transfer the title. The seller must also warrant that the horse is free of any security interest or lien of a third party (per Uniform Commercial Code). If a seller cannot warrant all of the above, then it should be carefully and conspicuously noted in the bill of sale which warranties are *not* made. For example, if a horse has changed hands several times and his papers are an irreconcilable mess but the buyer doesn't care because he is just buying him "AS IS" as a grade horse, then state that in your bill of sale in clear language. Consider using BOLD CAPITAL letters where the sale is referenced as "AS IS."

Remember (from chapter 7) that any statements of fact or promise by the seller can become part of the "basis of the bargain." So, as a seller, be very careful that you accurately represent what you are selling. If you are considered a horse professional and you say a horse will fit a particular purpose and the horse fails to do so, you may be held liable. "AS IS" indicates that no warranty is being conveyed and the buyer is accepting the horse for what he appears to be. WHAT YOU SEE IS WHAT YOU GET!

Chapter Thirteen

Alternatives to Selling

DONATION

Sometimes it is financially more reasonable to donate a horse to a school or non profit organization than sell him. If a horse is steady and sound, even though he may have some age on him, he may be valuable for a college or university riding program or to a handicapped riding association. In some cases, 4–H groups and Pony Club might also be able to accept donations. Be sure the organization is legitimate and that you have the right to check on the horse to be sure he is working out and is being well cared for. Also, have a written stipulation that if the organization wants to sell or give away the horse, you will be notified first.

Giving your horse to a nonprofit organization may allow you to deduct the fair market value of the horse from your income. Because such a donation is considered a charitable contribution, if you itemize your deductions, you might enjoy a tax benefit from your donation. If the value of the horse is over $5,000, a qualified appraisal might be required by the IRS. Check with your accountant or tax adviser on this issue.

LEASING

If you really don't want to sell your horse but you need help paying for his expenses, you might want to offer your horse on a full lease or a half-lease (share-a-horse).

Usually someone who agrees to a full lease expects to take the horse to her own facility and care for and use the horse exclusively. However, if you have the facilities and room but you just need help with costs, consider a full lease with you allowing the lessee to keep the horse at your place.

A horse on a shared lease would most likely reside at the owner's facility, and the half-lessee would share the costs and use of the horse.

TRADING

I've heard of some pretty wild trades that have been made involving horses. Trading can mean exchanging horses *or* swapping a horse for a boat or jewelry or . . . I'll leave the options to your imagination. Bartering is a good way for two people to exchange goods they no longer want or need without using cash.

EUTHANASIA

If the horse you have for sale is dangerous or is permanently unsound and he or she is not useful for breeding, you should consider having the animal humanely destroyed. Sending such a horse to a sale barn to be sold as a killer (meat) horse may not be a good idea for two reasons. First, if the horse is ill or injured, he will likely suffer during transport and handling. Second, if the horse has a hidden serious defect or dangerous behavior, someone might buy the horse hoping to use him for riding. You wouldn't want to be responsible for someone getting hurt or finding out they have an unsound animal on their hands. If a horse is at the end of the road, the responsible and kind thing to do is to arrange for humane euthanasia. Once a horse is dead, you will either have to bury him or have his body removed by a livestock disposal service. Horses can usually be buried on private land that is outside city limits, but if you have any doubts, call your local animal control office or the state department of health to be sure burial is legal. To bury, it will be necessary to hire a backhoe operator to dig a hole big enough for a horse. Arrangements should be made ahead of time because the body should be buried within a day or two of euthanasia.

Having the horse's body removed and taken to a rendering plant is a more common way of dealing with a horse carcass. It will cost you about $100 to have the horse picked up and delivered to the factory. The horse's carcass is converted to fertilizer or pet food.

RETIREMENT

If you find yourself with a dear old horse that you really can't part with, one that has given you years of service and friendship yet is unusable for riding or breeding, you may wish to consider retirement. Retirement is not dumping a horse out on a pasture and forgetting about him, however. Older horses require all the proper care and feed that horses in their prime need and, in some cases, more. It is unfair to turn a senior citizen out with rambunctious youngsters.

If you can provide good retirement care, all the better. But there are equine retirement farms popping up all over the country. Refer to the appendix for a few suggestions.

Appendix

RECOMMENDED READING

Equine Travelers of America, Inc. *Nationwide Overnight Stabling Directory*. Arkansas City, KS,1995. (*accommodations for horses across the United States, updated annually*)

Harris, Susan E. *Grooming to Win,* 2nd Ed. New York: Howell Book House, 1991. (*current show ring standards and breed requirements as well as health care and conditioning*)

Hill, Cherry. *Becoming an Effective Rider.* Pownal, VT: Garden Way, 1991. (*mental and physical development of the rider*)

———. *The Formative Years. Raising and Training the Horse from Birth to Two Years.* Ossining, NY: Breakthrough, 1988. (*extensive ground training, especially manners and restraint*)

———. *From the Center of the Ring: An Inside View of Horse Competitions.* Pownal, VT: Garden Way, 1988.

———. *Horsekeeping on a Small Acreage.* Pownal, VT: Garden Way, 1990. (*facilities design and management*)

———. *Making Not Breaking, The First Year Under Saddle.* Ossining, NY: Breakthrough, 1992.

———. *101 Arena Exercises*: *A Ringside Guide for Horse and Rider.* Pownal, VT: Garden Way, 1995.

Hill, Cherry, and Richard Klimesh. *Maximum Hoof Power: How to Improve Your Horse's Performance Through Proper Hoof Management.* New York: Howell Book House, 1994.

Johnson, George G. *In the Balance: The Horsemen's Guide to Legal Issues.* Golden, CO: Pica Publishing, 1993. (*written by an attorney-at-law*)

Marder, Sue Ellen, L.L.M. *Legal Forms, Contracts, and Advice for Horse Owners*. Ossining, NY: Breakthrough, 1991.

McAllister, Bruce. *Horse Travel Guide*. Boulder, CO: Roundup Press, 1995. (*accommodations for horses across the United States, updated annually*)

Stashak, Ted, D.V.M., and Cherry Hill. *Horseowner's Guide to Lameness*. Philadelphia: Lea & Febiger, 1995. (*extensive, thorough coverage of lameness signs, causes, treatment, and prevention*)

Strickland, Charlene. *Show Grooming*. Ossining, NY: Breakthrough, 1986.

Wood, Kenneth A., B.S., J.D. *Law for the Horse Breeder*. Phoenix, AZ: Farnum Equipment Co., updated 1994. (*legal, tax, contract, liability, sales*)

ADDITIONAL SOURCES OF INFORMATION

American Society of Equine Appraisers, P.O. Box 186, Twin Falls, ID 83303.

Brown's Performance Horses, 325 East County Road 56, Fort Collins, CO 80524; Phone (303) 493–0953. (*video sales of horses for barrel racing and roping*)

Cherry Hill Videos, P.O. Box 140, Livermore, CO 80536; *Horse for sale video. (Send for information)*

Compu-Horse, Inc., 11444 W. Olympic Blvd., Suite 1100, Los Angeles, CA 90064; phone (205) 995–0530; fax (800) 995–4757; (205) 995–0534. (*computer-based home marketing*)

Equestrian Network Services, Inc., 1491 River Park Drive, Suite 200, Sacramento, CA 95815; phone (916) 641–0004. (*computerized data and photo listing*)

Equine Listing, P.O. Box 30726, North Las Vegas, NV 89036–0726; phone (800) 734–6514. (*nationwide listing, primarily Quarter Horses*)

Equipoise, Equine Sales Video Database, P.O. Box 31, Kings Highway, Sugar Loaf NY 10981–0031; phone 800–952–4791; Internet E-Mail bfugett@ bix.com. (*video sales of jumping, eventing, and dressage horses with professionally filmed footage*)

Julie I. Fershtman, Attorney-at-Law. 30700 Telegraph Road, Suite 3475, Bingham Farms, MI 48025–4527, Phone (810) 644–8600 and Fax (810) 644–8344. (*special expertise in equine litigation, contracts, and insurance law*)

Horse Industry Directory, published annually by the American Horse Council, 1700 K Street NW, Suite 300, Washington DC 20006; phone (202) 296–4031. (*lists Thoroughbred sales companies, equine insurance companies, breed journals, and periodicals*)

Laurie Krause, 7571 Weld County Road 38, Johnstown, CO 80534; phone (303) 587–2055. (*youth and amateur instruction, training, and sales*)

National Microchip Horse Registry, P.O. Box 1700, Athens TX 75751; phone (800) 327–8679. (*electronic identification for animals*)

Segraves and Associates, (Dale Segraves), P.O. Box 161456, Fort Worth, TX 76161; phone (817) 599–8600. (*horse sale management, catalog and advertising design, appraisals*)

Talking Warmblood Classifieds, phone (613) 836–1614.

United States Department of the Interior, Bureau of Land Management, 18th and C Streets NW, Washington DC 20240; phone (202) 542–7780. Also, Adopt-A-Horse, Consumer Information Center, Pueblo CO 81009.

Veterinary Genetics Laboratory, School of Veterinary Medicine, University of California Davis, Davis, CA 95616–8744; phone (916) 752–2211. Also, American Quarter Horse Association, P.O. Box 200, Amarillo, TX 79168. (*HYPP testing*)

RETIREMENT FARMS

Thoroughbred Retirement Foundation Inc., Suite 351, 1050 State Highway 35, Shrewsbury, NJ 07702; phone (908) 957–0182.

California Equine Retirement Foundation, 34033 Kooden Road, Winchester CA 95296; mailing address P.O. Box 295, Temecula CA 95290; phone (909) 926–4190.

Ryerss Farm for Aged Equines, Ridge Road, RD 2, Pottstown PA 19464; phone (215) 469–0533.

Guide to Interstate Health Requirements

Each state establishes its own rules for animals entering its borders. These requirements are often amended. It is advisable to check with the state veterinarian at your destination prior to shipment. Regulations are in effect as of January 1995 and are reprinted by permission of the American Horse Council. *Note:* Alaska, Puerto Rico, and Canada did not respond to the American Horse Council's request for updated material by press time.

State	EIA Test Required	CVI*	Temp. Reading
Alabama	Yes (12 months) (B)	Yes	No
Alaska	Yes (6 months) (B)	Yes (ii, vii)	No
Arizona	No	Yes (v)	No
Arkansas	Yes (12 months) (B)	Yes	Yes
California	Yes (6 months) (B)	Yes (iii)	No
Canada	Yes (6 months)	Yes (iv)	Yes
Colorado	Yes (12 months) (H)	Yes	No
Connecticut	Yes (12 months)	Yes	No
Delaware	Yes (12 months) (B, D)	Yes	Yes
Florida	Yes (12 months) (B, C) †	Yes (v, vii)	Yes
Georgia	Yes (12 months) (B, C)	Yes	Yes
Hawaii	Yes (3 months)	Yes (i, vii) ***	No
Idaho	No	Yes	No
Illinois	Yes (12 months) (A)	Yes	No
Indiana	Yes (12 months) (C)	Yes	No
Iowa	Yes (12 months) (B)	Yes	No
Kansas	Yes (12 months) (B, C)	Yes	No
Kentucky	Yes (12 months) (B, C, D, G)	Yes	No**
Louisiana	Yes (12 months)	Yes	No
Maine	Yes (6 months) (B)	Yes (vi)	No
Maryland	Yes (12 months) (B)	Yes (i)	No**
Massachusetts	Yes (6 months) (B)	Yes	Yes
Michigan	Yes (6 months)	Yes	No
Minnesota	Yes (12 months) (B, H)	Yes	No
Mississippi	Yes (12 months) (G)	Yes	No
Missouri	Yes (12 months) (B, C)	Yes (vii)	No
Montana	No (E)	Yes (ii)	No
Nebraska	Yes (12 months) (E)	Yes	No
Nevada	Yes (6 months) (B, C, G)	Yes	No
New Hampshire	Yes (6 months) (G)	Yes	No
New Jersey	Yes (12 months) (B)	Yes	No
New Mexico	Yes (12 months) (B)	Yes	No
New York	Yes (12 months)	Yes (vii)	No
North Carolina	Yes (12 months) (B)	Yes	No
North Dakota	Yes (12 months) (E,C)	Yes	No
Ohio	Yes (6 months) (A)	Yes	Yes
Oklahoma	Yes (6 months) (A)	Yes	No
Oregon	Yes (6 months) (B)	Yes (ii)	No
Pennsylvania	Yes (12 months) (B, C, G)	Yes	No
Puerto Rico	Yes (6 months)	Yes (i, vii)	No
Rhode Island	No ***	Yes (i)	Yes
South Carolina	Yes (12 months) (B)	Yes	No

South Dakota	Yes (12 months) (B)	Yes	No
Tennessee	Yes (12 months) (B, D)	Yes	No
Texas	Yes (12 months) (A, C, G)	Yes (ii, v, vii)	No
Utah	Yes (12 months)	Yes(v)	No
Vermont	Yes (12 months) (B)	Yes	No
Virginia	Yes (12 months)	Yes	No
Washington	Yes (6 months)(B)	Yes	No
West Virginia	Yes (6 months) (F)	Yes	No
Wisconsin	Yes (6 months) (C)	Yes	No
Wyoming	Yes (12 months) (B, C)	Yes	No

† When EIA test is required, laboratory name and address, accession number and test date with results must be included.

* Certificate of Veterinary Inspection (CVI) filed with the State Veterinarian in state of origin are required.

** Recommended.

*** Under revision.

Footnotes - EIA Testing:

(A) EIA test required for equine over 12 months of age.

(B) EIA test required for equine less than 12 months of age. For age requirement, contact the state veterinarian's office. Wyoming: no pending EIA test allowed.

(C) Suckling foals accompanying EIA-negative dams are exempt. Wyoming: no pending EIA test allowed.

(D) EIA test required within 6 months for sale or auction.

(E) EIA test required for equine from certain states. For specific states contact state veterinarian.

(F) 12 months if state of origin has a state EIA program.

(G) Test chart must accompany animal. Some states require original copy.

(H) Permit required if EIA test is pending when horse is shipped.

(I) Permit and EIA test required for National Rodeo Finals.

Footnotes Certificate of Veterinary Inspection (CVI).

(i) Pre-approved CVI from state of origin required prior to shipment. Required in Michigan on imported exhibition equine only.

(ii) Permit from the state of destination is required prior to entry. Texas: slaughter horses only.

(iii) Copy of CVI and $2 filing fee must be sent to CA by date of shipment.

(iv) U.S. origin CVI, endorsed by a USDA approved veterinarian, valid 30 days from date of inspection.

(v) Complete description of horse including brands or tatoos.

(vi) Approved copy of CVI must be submitted to state veterinarian's office after entry.

(vii) State has requirements regarding vaccinations, testing or other.

Index